Love, you should've had my back

by Quaneysha S. Poindexter

This book is contains 98% of actual events

Love, you should've had my back

Note for Librarians: A cataloguing record for this book is available from Library and Archives
Canada at www.collectionscanada.ca/amicus/index-e.html
ISBN 1-4120-8511-x

Printed on paper with minimum 30% recycled fibre.
Trafford's print shop runs on "green energy" from solar, wind and other environmentally-friendly power sources.

TRAFFORD
PUBLISHING™
Offices in Canada, USA, Ireland and UK

Book sales for North America and international:
Trafford Publishing, 6E–2333 Government St.,
Victoria, BC V8T 4P4 CANADA
phone 250 383 6864 (toll-free 1 888 232 4444)
fax 250 383 6804; email to orders@trafford.com
Book sales in Europe:
Trafford Publishing (UK) Limited, 9 Park End Street, 2nd Floor
Oxford, UK OX1 1HH UNITED KINGDOM
phone 44 (0)1865 722 113 (local rate 0845 230 9601)
facsimile 44 (0)1865 722 868; info.uk@trafford.com
Order online at:
trafford.com/06-0266

10 9 8 7 6 5 4 3 2 1

Love, you should've had my back

Dedicated to:
my mother, my fiancée,
my family, and friends.
Love you all!

Love, you should've had my back

Author's Page

Quaneysha Poindexter grew up in New Haven, Connecticut. She was the only child to Deidre Poindexter. Her father, Wesley Williams abandoned her when she was born and then tried to reappear back in her life; only to again disappear when she was in high school. Being the only girl amongst a bunch of boys, she became a tomboy. Her mother raised her to the best of her ability, often restricting her from hanging out. She did her best to provide for her and keep food in the house; sometimes behind in bills to keep her daughter up to par. She instilled important values and lessons in her, ones that would follow and aide her throughout life. Because Quaneysha was not permitted to live the life she wanted as a teenager, she rebelled against her mother. She turned to the streets and peers in high school, which ultimately led her down the wrong path. She engaged in sex, drugs, and other activities her mother would not have approved of.

Though she did some things in her life she would later regret, she was a smart young woman. Her mother encouraged her to finish school and become a better person than she was. Quaneysha loved to write and later on in high school she decided she wanted to become a journalist. She also loved music just as equal as she loved to write. In an effort to fulfill both her likings, her dream was to become a writer for a renowned hip-hop magazine company and interview celebrities. She pursued her dream by becoming a writer in her school's newspaper, "The Sentinel."

Because she made the choice to become involved with boys, her dreams were put on hold. Although she was accepted to five colleges, one in which offered her $19,000 in financial aid, she decided she would stay in her home town for a year to work and get extra money; that was a big mistake. She attended college for about a week, only to withdraw after 9-11. After her withdrawal, she became involved in the streets more and began selling drugs. After one too many close calls with death, she decided to call it quits.

Since she never had a father in her life, she never had a man around to show her how she should be treated by a man. Luckily her mother instilled values in her or else she would have let men use and abuse her. She finally met her sole mate after being hurt numerous times by boys who wanted nothing more from her than sex. Though she found true love in her life, she had to deal with the pain that came with it. Ultimately making her a stronger woman, along with the values her mother instilled in her, she shares her life story with the world in her book, *Love, you should've had my back*.

She currently resides in Atlanta, GA and attends the University of Phoenix's Gwinnett campus for Business Management/Marketing. Once she is done with her schooling, she plans on using her degree to manage her own business(es) and create better jobs for everyone, so look out for her in a town near you.

Love, you should've had my back

Acknowledgements

First and foremost I would like to thank God. Without him I would have no sense of direction. Thank you. I also would like to thank my mother. Without you mom, I have no life. You made me see my potential and my talent. You showed me that writing was indeed my talent and now we both can reap the benefits of you raising a good young lady. Thank you for being there for me through thick and thin and thank you for being patient with me. You may not like any of these events but it is my life. I am not regretful because I turned it into a positive thing, but I just want you to know that anything I did in the past was not done to hurt you.

To my fiancée, I love you so much. Without you, I probably would have never written a book. I will never forget you and I would never play you. Love you always and forever.

To my peeps, you know who you are. Dee and Ronisha, hold it down, keep it real and do away with all the phoney shit (and you know what I'm talking about). Thanks for sharing your problems with me because it also made the book. Dee, thanks for becoming friends with me because without you, I may have never met your brother. Make the right decisions and leave the bum niggas alone.

Marquiesce, thanks for being there like no other. Your friendship has been invaluable in my life and you have done so much for me that I do not know how to repay you. Stay keeping it real with me and you know I will look out for you little sis. I'll do my best to introduce you to Banks if I meet him (laugh). Make the right decisions and hold your head.

To the siblings I never had, Cherish, Keith Jr., Elijah, Carol, and Charday. Hold your head and strive to be the best you can be. Don't let anyone stand in the way of your success and remember to make the right decisions in life. Love Ya'll. To my father-in-law Keith Sr., hold your head, you will be home soon.

To my immediate family, Grandma Lottie, my cousin who is like my sister, Teysha, my brother Wesley, my aunts Daphine and Dawn, my uncles Jermaine, and especially my Uncle Mel in the fed jail – hold your head uncle, you'll be home soon, Love you. To my other cousins, love ya'll too.

To my step family, auntie Margaret, Delores, Gwen, Sheryl, Rosa, and Grandma Mccrea, thanks for accepting me in the family and thanks for raising a gentleman.

And anybody else who I may have forgotten who are close to me, thanks for being in my life. Also, to everyone who inspired me to write the book and believed in me at the highest level, thank you so much for your love and support.

Love, you should've had my back

Some of my family may not like some of the things I have done in my life but it is my life. Things happen for a reason, and my reason, though I couldn't see it back then, was to expose my true talent – writing. There are many people out there who have done worse things than me. That's life and this is my life, it is what it is; so as Mary J. Blige said in one of her songs, "take me as I am, or have nothing at all."

To all the haters out there, like 50 cent say, "I need you…I need you to hate… So I could use you for your energy." Controversy sells, so keep me on your mind (laugh).

To Keyshia Cole, thanks for putting out an excellent album. You inspired me to use your song title of one of my favorite songs, as my book title. I wanted to use the whole song title but I didn't want you coming to sue me (laugh).

Oh and shout out to my deadbeat father, Wesley Williams, thanks for not being there for me pops and all your other kids at that. It's all good though, you're gonna get yours one day and you will know why. (laugh)

And finally, thank you everyone who purchased this book. You definitely got your monies worth, I promise. One!

Though many may judge me and say what they want to say, only God can judge me. Like Mary J. said, "I put it out there so you could feel me, so you could know the real me". This is my life and I am not running from it, it is what it is.

Preface

What is Love? Webster's dictionary defines love as a strong affection; warm attachment; an attraction based on sexual desire; an unselfish loyal and benevolent concern for others; to feel a passion, devotion, or tenderness for; to love is to cherish. BULLSHIT! Love is a deadly game, or at least real true authentic love. Not love that you think you may feel but rather love that is mutual. Don't get me wrong, it's beautiful to be in love with someone, and everyone should experience it at least once in their life, but this can be the most dangerous emotion known to mankind, and not too many make it out alive – literally. It's a game of survival of the fittest.

When you meet a person, you're never expecting to fall in love with them. In fact, had you known, you probably would have told him or her you weren't interested when they offered to buy you that drink and ultimately changed your life. We cannot predict the future, that's what makes life interesting because we never know what's behind the door ahead. Our mind can play tricks on us; what we think is love, can just be our desire to be loved by the opposite sex. The initial meeting with REAL love is obscured. You don't know you're in love until something goes wrong and you realize you can't live without that person, regardless of how harsh the situation. You may say, *well how will I know I'm in a mutual loving situation?* Trust me…you'll know.

All men say women are no good, and all women say men are no good. The truth of the matter is that men have been dogs since the beginning of time, when kings would have more than one wife at the same time. Cheating is just in a man's nature. Women, on the other hand, actually adapt this behavior from the men after being in love with a man who broke her heart. Arguably, this is where women adapt the phrase, *she ain't shit*. In the world we live in today, we have the double standard bullshit. A man who has sex with thirty women is a hero, but a woman who has sex with even ten men is a hoe. What's the big deal? If a woman is single, why can't she get her shit off? Women have a high hormonal level just as men do, if not higher. Well I'm here to tell all my women, if you are single and you find a man attractive and you would like to have sex with him; fuck him and fuck him good. Just know that he will not make you his wife if you're fucking him and the next man. He will also probably not make you his wife if you fuck him on the first night. And ladies, play it safe. There are too many diseases out there; you must treat every man as if they are infected with something. Not only that, you don't want to sleep with multiple men simultaneously, get pregnant and don't know who your baby's father is; you will look really stupid if that happens. Sleep with one man at a time and do it safely because if he is not your man, he is most likely sleeping with other women. And don't go around sucking anybody's dick; not only is that risky also, but that's when you become a hoe.

      To all the men and women, if after reading this book I wasn't able to prevent you from hurting the one you love, then I have failed myself. God never gives us anything we cannot handle in life; but don't get it twisted, we can get ourselves in shit we cannot handle. As Keyshia Cole said, "sometimes in life, you know… situations come your way… you just gotta make good decisions man… you gotta know your focus in life…and if love is your focus…then man…pay attention."

We all make mistakes, but before you make a mistake that may haunt you the rest of your life, think about it ten times. Sometimes just thinking about it can prevent you from doing it. This book may also change your mind about finding the love of your life, but you cannot run from it; it will find you just as death will. However, some people will also be curious about love after reading this book. Just remember this one thing, "Curiosity killed the cat – satisfaction brought it back." The choice is yours! I'm only twenty-two, but damn it's been rough. Walk wit' me!

Love, you should've had my back

Introduction: From Beginning to End

He's crawling on his knees begging for forgiveness as he's clinging to her legs, shedding tears as he wished he could rewind time and not have cheated for the second time.

"I'm sorry boo, I love you. You are who I want to spend my life with. You are the one I have built everything with, not anyone else. You are the one with the ring. Please don't leave me." Why do they all do this shit? They cheat, thinking they can get away with it and then when they get caught they want to beg you not to leave them; you forgive them, but then they cheat again. If they love you so much, why do they jeopardize the relationship by cheating in the first place; let alone cheat over and over. Okay, once may be forgiven – it can be accepted as a mistake – but if it happens again, it's no longer considered a mistake. Everyone can say they would do this and do that to someone who cheated on them, but reality is, you don't know what you will do until you get in that situation, especially if you really love that person. Many people would call a woman who stayed with a man after he cheated multiple times, a "fool," but we can't control our affection and feelings over the opposite sex; knowledge of ourselves help us to decide what is enough to let go no matter how much you may not want to.

So here in this small room, she stared him in the eyes and said, "I thought you loved me. I forgave you the first time and now you do it again. Now what am I supposed to do?"

"Baby, I was drunk. She was all over me, I wasn't thinking."

1

"You said the same shit before. The fucking bitch was all over you and you couldn't help yourself. So every bitch that throws herself on you can basically get MY dick." That was her biggest concern, the fact that another chick got a piece of what was supposed to belong to her. She was the one there through thick and thin, she was the one who did everything for him, not any other chick.

"No baby, I'm sorry. I drunk too much liquor."

"You really expect me to buy that huh? Liquor is no excuse. If you get drunk to the point you don't know what's going on, then you shouldn't be drinking."

They say you never realize what you have until you don't have it anymore. Well she should have left his ass out in the cold when he pulled this bullshit the first time and maybe he would have learned his lesson. But she felt deep down inside that the man she dreamed of who would fill the loss of love and affection from a man (due to absence of a father), would never cheat on her in the first place; but you can't put things past people. To avoid disappointment, always expect the worst, especially with men. The first time she accepted him cheating as a mistake, but then he did the shit again. What made him think he could just keep fucking bitches, beg her back, and everything would be all good? I guess he thought she'd always be there for him since technically she was "wifey" and all the others were his "jump-offs." No! That doesn't fly either. He could dish it, but I bet a million dollars he couldn't take it if she gave his "pussy" away. And believe me, she could have. There were many times when she was drunk and wanted to experience some "new" dick.

"Baby please. I know I fucked up, but I love you. There's no doubt about that, anyone can see that. Don't do this to me. Please."

"Don't do this to you? Don't do this to you? That's all you fucking think about is you. You, you, you. There's more to life than

2

just you motherfucker.   You should have thought about me when you laid down with these bitches."

"I did think of you."

"Well what the fuck did you think? That she or rather they, were me? Or oh, let me guess, you thought I wouldn't find out huh? You are a fucking disgrace. You walk around here all innocent like you not like all these other dudes, when in fact you are no different." The innocent ones are the ones you have to watch out for; they are worse than all others. Their game is so tight that they fool you into thinking they're totally different. They get you to open your heart to them, and then they prove you wrong. Now there was no doubt in her mind that he didn't love her because if there were, she definitely would not have stayed with him the first time. Truth be told, he did love her. Anytime a man has butterflies from the threat of his woman leaving him and can't eat and sleep, he's definitely in love. They both felt like they were each other's sole mate. So what was the problem? I guess the most logical explanation was that he was a man and that would explain his behavior. For some reason a man just can't say no. They just can't let a hard dick go to waste. They have to use it on any woman in their sight. The sad thing is, for some men, she doesn't even have to be attractive; as they say, "they all look the same when the lights go out." Well he fucked up now. He had no idea what was in store for him.

"I can't do this shit anymore. I can't stress myself, I'll mess around and die messing with you. I went through this same ordeal with you over a year ago. You just didn't learn, huh? What you thought? You thought I wouldn't find out again huh? You stupid as fuck."

She was now on the verge of slapping the shit out of him. The only problem was, she was one hundred pounds less than him.

She damn sure wasn't going to battle with a 215 pound man; she refused to have another occurrence of what happened before. As she started pointing in his face, she couldn't help but think how good her man looked. He had a fresh Caesar with his goatee nicely trimmed. She also knew if she took him back this time, the make-up sex would be off the chain. And she also knew she would have him eating out the palm of her hand. Unfortunately, she couldn't help but wonder how he fucked another bitch. Did he give it to her like she got it every night? Slow and passionate until she climaxed and bit the shit out of his neck cause he fucked her so well? Or did he put her on the bathroom sink and thrust at her pelvis like he was about to do a sixty-year bid and was never going to get to fuck again? What did he do? Did he get the bitch whipped and now she kept blowing him up to do it again? Or even worse, did she put it on him and now he couldn't let go? Shit, did he even use a condom? All the shit going around, that was too risky to forgive. And after the first incident, she hoped he learned his lesson and used one. At this point, his good looks and charm didn't even matter; it actually made it worse. She had so many thoughts running through her mind she didn't know what to do.

"Why you looking at me like that?" He said curiously as she gave him a look like he was her worse enemy. She walked away mumbling, *I got something for yo ass, you wanna fucking play me. Fuck that.* He just sat, shaking his head and sighing. She appeared three minutes later and all he heard was a *click/clack* sound. He turned around only to see her standing in the doorway with her baby glock.

"I love you baby. I always did. I never cheated on you. I gave you my all but I guess that wasn't good enough. If I can't be with you, nobody can."

4

"Baby please, don't do this. Think about what you're doing, we can work it out, but this won't solve anything."

"NO, fuck that, we can't work shit out." As tears began rolling down her baby face, she knew she couldn't put the gun down or he would probably kill her for pointing a gun at him, even though it wasn't the first time; but he knew this time she was serious considering the harshness of the situation. As he inched closer to her, she fired a warning shot just past his shoulder. "I'm not fucking playing with you." By this point, she had sparked someone to call 911 citing a strange *boom* sound.

"Yo what the fuck is wrong with you? Please calm down. Think about what you are doing. You all I got and I'm all you got, we a family and family stick together.

"You thought about your family when you was in that pussy? No. So why should I?"

"You don't have to do this. Please baby, please."

"It's too late to cop a plea. I told you I was crazy about you. You should have believed me."

"And you know I'm crazy about you. I love you. I swear. I'm a man, we make mistakes." I'm a man? What kind of excuse was that? He didn't know that dug him a deeper hole just for being a man.

"Sorry boo, I love you, but I can't do this anymore."

"Fuck it, do what you gotta do." He stared at her for about ten seconds and then dodged for the gun. *Bang, bang.* He died instantly. Shot in the head twice as he tried to wrestle for the gun and made her nervous. Would she really had shot him? Probably not. If anything, she would have wanted to still see him alive and miserable without her. She didn't even cry as she saw him drop.

5

"Put the gun down ma'am." She heard from behind her. It was the cops, who heard the gunshots coming in. She turned around with the gun still in her hand which was now pointing their way. *Bang, bang, bang.* They shot her dead because they thought she would shoot them. She dropped right beside her man. They both died behind four letters, L-O-V-E. Let's rewind to the beginning.

Chapter One: From the Beginning

When you meet a person, you never realize the impact they will have on your life. Meeting a new friend can seem so innocent, like *it's just a new friend,* but that can play a major role in your life. That was definitely the case when Dalani Jackson met Marie Hall. It was sixth grade at the local junior high school. The way Dalani, or Lani for short, met Marie or rather Marie met Lani, was strange. Supposedly Lani walked by Marie's desk, passed gas, the two laughed and clicked from then on. They may have clicked but they weren't close in junior high. Marie had another friend whom she grew up with; LaNisha Graham, or Nisha for short, was also a friend of Lani's from elementary school. Nisha was more close to Marie than Lani, so Lani never really hung with the two. She was never allowed to hang anyway because her mother kept her secluded.

Lani was always a good student. When she was born, the doctor said she would be retarded. They were wrong as usual. She had an unusual intelligence, far more knowledgeable than her peers. The majority of her teachers loved her and knew she had more potential than what she gave, but she chose to be a class clown most of the time. She wanted to impress her peers. She would do crazy things in school that would probably have supported the aforementioned assumption the doctors made. The kids in her class probably thought she was weird, but she did those things for popularity. She didn't want to be considered an "egghead," "bookworm," or a "nerd." She wanted to be the smart kid who got

7

good grades and was also considered "live." When she was in the second grade, her teachers tried to skip her to the third grade, but her mother wasn't too fond of that. She didn't want her to skip any education, even if she already knew it. She wanted to ensure her daughter learned and understood everything before advancing. She loved to write and her mother would always tell her she had a writing talent. She would often write poems and share them with her mother and she also communicated with her mother through letters when they had disagreements since she was afraid to share her feelings verbally. She caught on to things quickly and was able to get along with most.

She never really had her father in her life. He would pop up once every "black" moon, even though at one point she lived right around the corner from him. He claimed he was on drugs really bad and didn't want her to see him like that, but even after he got himself cleaned, he still didn't come around. So she never really had that father figure in her life and we all know that can be devastating for a female; the young woman went looking for love in all in the wrong places. It's a shame that men don't realize what it does to a young girl who doesn't have a father. A young boy without a father (though no child should be left fatherless) is not as severe because a man is going to do what he has to do to survive anyway; but a female needs that man in her life to guide her in the right path and let her know how a real man should treat a woman so she could distinguish between what was right in a relationship, and what was wrong. Therefore, Lani grew up with only her mother in life, which was all she needed.

Her father was not a bad looking guy. He was light-skinned, medium build and had nice skin. He was not a good dresser and he did not have style. He was very different from the men her mother dealt with after him, as they had something to offer besides looks.

8

She never really knew her grandparents for the most part, or her uncles and aunts on his side of the family for that matter. She met her grandparents once or twice and all she knew was that her grandmother was blind. Of all her birthdays, she only remembered her father coming to one party when she was eleven years old. Her mother threw her a party at her aunt's house and he showed up. She didn't know how he knew about it, but he did show up and gave her one hundred dollars. He must have come across some money and was probably in his rehab stages because that was the first and only thing she ever received from him.

Her mother adored her and always wanted to protect her. Besides, she was her mother's only child. She kept her locked down in the house most of the time to assure her daughter was indeed protected from the temptations of the streets. Being a single parent and all, she did the best she could to provide for her. She wanted Lani to have nice things in life and she did her best to ensure she did, even if it meant skipping payments on bills to provide for her. There were times when all they had to eat were eggs in the fridge, and then there were times when it just looked like Thanksgiving. If it was one thing her mother knew, she knew she would stay dedicated to her daughter no matter how hard the times were. And her staying dedicated to her daughter meant not turning to drugs to diffuse her problems; she was not going to be a drug addict when she had a child to look after, and she didn't even bring that kind of stuff around Lani.

Her mother always emphasized the importance of her finishing high school, whether she attended college or not. As with any parent, she did want her daughter to attend college and further her education to make her more marketable and financially stable; but she was not going to press the issue if that was something Lani did not want to do. Her only concern was that her daughter got a high school diploma. That stuck with Lani throughout her youth and that was the one thing she wanted to do to make her mom happy if she didn't do anything else.

Lani was showered with nothing but love and support from her mother throughout life. Her mother not only loved her child, but also children in general. More so that she wanted to start a daycare but felt it was too much to pursue. And she was the one to not only trust with children, but also put them in order. There was something about her that kids just knew she wasn't the one to play with. She was not the type to laugh when a child cursed, or when a child hit her. She had one general rule, "don't leave your kids with me if you don't want me to discipline them." Her mother would always be in her corner, right or wrong. When she was wrong, she would be told about it and they would work it out together. If she was right, you better believe anybody else involved would hear it regardless of who they were or how they felt.

Lani also had two uncles who adored her. There was something special about Lani that made everyone cling to her. Her youngest uncle, especially, always wanted to protect her, but because he was in and out of jail, he was never able to do that. Her second uncle was just the opposite of his brother. He was smart, dark, and handsome. He was quiet and discreet about whatever it was he did. He was so discreet, the family was shocked when he was arrested by federal officials for conspiracy to sell drugs and handed him thirty-years. Lani was just eleven years old when her uncle was sent away to fed jail in upstate New York. He was really the one who she looked at as a father figure, and for him to go away, did not sit right with her.

Her eldest aunt was the church lady of the family. Since the family had hostility towards one another for various reasons and only came together for special occasions, she kept prayer over the family. She was the one who took the children to church every Sunday if she didn't do anything else. No matter how much the kids hated going to church, partly because of the long service that came with it, they had no choice but to go. And Lani hated it more than anyone. Although she believed in God, she did not like the idea of people jumping around and speaking in tongues; that just wasn't something she was into. She felt people could praise God without having to give their money. She was sure she could do the same thing the pastor was doing in the comfort of her own home (by herself) and get the same results. So it wasn't a disappointment to her when the only pastor they ever knew scammed the church for money and escaped to the south; that only helped her in her quest to cut ties with the church altogether. After that incident though, she did not like church at all because she felt people were using the Lord's name in vain and she did not want to have any part in that. She vowed to never step foot in a church again, and she kept her word.

No matter how much her mother tried to persuade her to stay away from men, that message did not serve its purpose. "Don't be like me, finish school, get your education, and then start a relationship. Boys are always going to be there," she would always say. Her mother gave birth to her at fifteen, so she did not want her daughter to go through the struggles of having a child and still being a child; especially being a single parent. Unfortunately, it didn't happen that way. Her mother was very strict on her. Lani knew better than to do a lot of things as a child. If there were grown ups in the house, she knew better than to be up in their face unless she was asked to be there. She knew not to be in grown folks business, and if she didn't know, her mother would be sure to give her that "look" to refresh her memory. She was so locked down, when she was able to go out in the world, she would show her ass; but only to the people who she knew wouldn't tell her mother on her, like her older cousin. When she hung with her, she knew she could do just about anything and get away with it. If she didn't get away with it, her cousin wouldn't tell her mother on her, she would just take it upon herself and discipline Lani. Lani loved music and she loved to dance. Not only did she find dancing amusing, but the people she would dance for also found her dancing style amusing, rather than an art.

When she was born, she wasn't the cutest baby and her own mother told her that once she got older. If anyone thought to be phoney and tell Lani's mother her daughter was "pretty," she would tell them to stop lying. She was very light and pale with patches of hair on her head. As she grew older, her looks began to come in and her mother kept braids in her hair so her hair could grow. Some of the boys in junior high would call her "alien three-head" because she had a big forehead. And when the snowfall came, she did not like to walk by the crowd of young boys because they would always throw snowballs at her. She didn't feel beautiful at all in junior high. Though she felt this way, she did have her share of boys in junior high school into high school. Though she did not lose her virginity until high school, she did have "puppy love" with a few boys in junior high. She got her first taste of how boys were in sixth grade when she finally got a chance to have a conversation with the boy she had a crush on for weeks. Even before that though, she had a deep connection with a young boy named Derek, whom she really liked as a child; but they were separated when he went to another school.

The minute she got on the phone with Cuda, all he was trying to do was come over. She liked him so much that she completely disregarded the fact that he just wanted to "hit it." It just so happened that her mom wasn't home one day, so she thought, *what the hell.* Even though she didn't like that this young boy, who was the same age as her, was so fast – cause all she wanted to do was talk to him over the phone and possibly kiss him – she invited him over. She waited and waited but he never showed. And fortunately for her he didn't because she probably may have lost her virginity in the sixth grade, at only eleven years old. He was probably frontin' anyway to see what she would say. Or maybe he was scared. *Maybe he just wasn't interested,* she thought to herself. That was just the first sample of the type of guys she would encounter in her life.

She was young anyway. She shouldn't have been trying to get up with no dude. Besides, if her mother had found out, she would have beat that ass so bad, she would have thought ten times before being sneaky. That didn't stop her though; she was very attracted to the opposite sex. There were even times when she was caught by one of her cousins, kissing her "boyfriend." She was afraid because she thought her cousin would tell her mother, but it never leaked out. Wayne was probably her deepest "love" as a child in junior high, and she was even heartbroken when he moved to a different school and lost connections with him.

Marie and Nisha had it good and Lani wanted to be down. They were able to hang out at a young age without strict discipline from their parents. They went to the neighborhood parties and were able to hang out after school. Not Lani though, she had to go straight home after school. That's just the way it was going to be, no if, ands, or buts about it. And who could blame her mom? She was only eleven years old talking about partying. That just wasn't the kind of environment her mother wanted to expose her to at such an early age. Her mother was young before, so she knew the type of things that went on at parties amongst young children who didn't know any better and had no parental supervision. But Lani would front to her friends like she wasn't on lockdown. *Yeah I'll hang out with ya'll after school*, she would say to them, knowing in her mind, she wasn't going anywhere. If they asked why she didn't show up, she would just make up a good excuse as to why she couldn't hang with them, after a while, they would just stop asking.

Lani was always a tomboy. Since she was born she did masculine things. She would climb fences, trees, etc... She was the only child to her mother, but she had many cousins – the majority males. She didn't like shoes, dresses, skirts, none of that. Since she basically grew up around males, it wasn't a shock when she decided to play basketball for her school. She wasn't a bad player either. Basketball was her first love as a youngster. She honestly believed that one day she would make it to the WNBA. She touched up her skills each year and became better. Her last year in junior high, she was apart of a winning girl's basketball team, who had an undefeated record of 13-0.

She was now graduating junior high. She had no idea of the years ahead as she entered high school. Not only did that mean another four years of school, but also four years to mature, become responsible, and also decide which way she wanted her life to go. She was never aware of the difficult challenge she was about to face.

Chapter Two: FRESH MEAT

Lani attended James Hillhouse High School in New Haven, Connecticut, her home town. Before she entered high school, she had heard rumors that many students in that school and also their rival school, Wilbur Cross, had a very high rate of AIDS amongst the students. Around this time, Lani didn't know too much about AIDS. Although her mother told her a little about it, she never knew about AIDS in depth. She also didn't believe the hype. Although the informants would state that the school kept statistics, that wasn't very convincing for her to leave boys alone altogether.

At the beginning of the freshman year, Lani was nervous. As any other youngster entering high school, she was shy and quiet. It was a new beginning, new friends to meet, more things to do and there was really no one to hang out with. Marie was at a different school, and her and Nisha weren't that close yet. She did eventually meet new friends and found her niche, but it was definitely an adjustment for her. She would eventually play for her high school girls' basketball team to buy some time.

She still wasn't able to do the things Marie and Nisha were doing. If anything, her mother became stricter when her daughter entered high school. LeAidra Jackson, or Lee as they called her, knew high school was dangerous, especially for "fresh meat," so she was really locked down; besides, Lee only wanted the best for her daughter. So to escape her prison cell, Lani participated in so-called school activities; but basketball was her only extra-curricular activity.

15

During her first year, she became even more aroused and influenced by boys, probably because of the variety and maturity she was presented with. She would flirt a lot and go to the boys' basketball games to see their dicks poking through their shorts; wondering how a particular boy stroked it or how big his dick was. She was definitely in her prime (or at least she thought she was). She was actually in the stage most girls her age were in – the *I think I'm grown, you can't tell me nothing* stage. She also became more educated than ever, not just about academics, but also life itself and the streets. Her mother could teach her a lot, but her environment taught her much more. The reason for that is that most parents want to keep the harsh reality hidden from their children, but when other [grown] kids know what's going on and pass that information to those who don't have knowledge about a particular subject; it makes that person more informative and knowledgeable. And the environment was how Lani learned much of her information.

At this point in her life, she was fed up with being restricted from living her youth. She wanted to go places with her friends, or even sneak off with a boy. She was fed up with telling her friends lies about why she couldn't hang with them. She finally said "fuck it" and took matters into her own hands. One day after basketball practice, she didn't go home. Instead, she went to one of her teammates' home to have some fun. Although what she was doing was innocent – she wasn't with a boy, she wasn't doing drugs – her mother didn't know that. In fact, Lee didn't know where her daughter was. Back then, not too many kids had cell phones.

She was too busy enjoying her evening that she didn't stop to think about what her mother was thinking about. She knew in the back of her mind as soon as her mother saw her, no matter where she saw her, she was going to get her ass whooped. She didn't care though, at least not while she was enjoying herself. She felt she was already in trouble, so why not enjoy the rest of the evening.

It was now 10 o'clock at night. Lee hadn't seen her daughter since she left for school at eight in the morning. For all she knew, her daughter was dead. On the way home, she couldn't help but think about how that ass whipping would feel. She was wishing the ride home could be longer, but of course it wasn't, every light was green.

As she arrived at her house, she hurried out the car so her mother wouldn't come out the house and embarrass her. She said her goodbyes to her friend and her friend's mother (and she probably really meant goodbye) and hurried them off so they wouldn't be outside waiting to make sure she got in. She approached the door, heart-pounding and thinking of what to tell her mother. As she put the key in, she felt the lock turn by itself. It was her mother, opening the door before she could.

"Where the fuck have you been?" Lee said grabbing Lani's jaws.

"I was at my friend's house."

"Your friend who?"

"Her name is Kia. I play basketball with her."

"So why you didn't call me to say something? I didn't know what happened to you. I didn't know if you got kidnapped, killed, anything." Lee began crying. She loved her daughter to death and just wanted to protect her. Lani was all she had to look forward to, the reason she wanted to wake up everyday; she wanted to be the best parent she could. Lani felt bad, but at the same time, she was tired, she didn't want a lecture, she just wanted whatever she was going to get. She also felt that if her mother would allow her to do these things and didn't make her fearful of her, she could call her and

17

let her know where she was. After babbling for about three more minutes, Lani finally got what she was waiting for, the ass whooping of her life – and that it most certainly was. As any other teenager, however, it would not be the last of incidents like this one.

The next day as Lani was getting ready for school, Lee burst into her room. Lani thought it was the rest of her ass whooping, but Lee just wanted to give her some advice. "Try me again today if you want. You come straight home from school. No basketball, no nothing. Don't make me come to that school and embarrass you." And if that's what she said, that's what she meant. She would go to the school and embarrass her if she felt Lani didn't respect her authoritative method of parenting. Lani was a bit upset because she loved basketball and that was her only escape route to another life other than the one behind the doors of her home. She was angry her mother took that away from her, regardless of the fact that if she missed practice, she would either not play in the next game, or she would possibly get kicked off the team. Although she deserved it, she contemplated her next move. She didn't want to disobey Lee because the last thing she wanted was to be embarrassed and talked about in the whole school, yet on the other hand, she didn't want to be kicked off the team. Knowing Lani, she was going to make up something. Besides she was a Leo, born in August and August is another word for majestic.

When dismissal came, she felt it best to just go home. She told her coach she had a family emergency and was excused for it. She just hoped Lee would let her return to practice the next day since she obeyed her and went straight home. Although Lee was upset with her, she felt it necessary she and her daughter have a talk because somewhere in the past their lines of communication got crossed; even though the majority of their means of communication

18

consisted of letters written back and forth to each other because for some reason they just couldn't say what they wanted to say to each other face to face.

"Lani, you know you were wrong for what you did last night." Her mother expressed with a mean look on her face. "You didn't have to worry me like that. All you had to do was call me and let me know you were at a friends' house. I have no problem with that, all I want you to do is call me and let me know you're okay, that's all." Lani just sat there as usual, she never really responded after her mother talked. That was just her usual procedure when it came to expressing her feelings verbally to her mother. She never really felt comfortable with talking to her being that she was so strict on her. She didn't want to say the wrong thing and get backslapped for it, so she just shut up. Although her mother told her she had no problem with her hanging out, Lani didn't trust that too much. Besides, her mother wanted her to call her any time she left from a place she was originally. So any time she would leave one friends' house to go anywhere else, she had to inform her mother. Since none of her other friends did that with their parents, she didn't want to do that with hers. Though she did try communicating with her mother on a few occasions, she didn't like her mother calling numbers back when it got too late; she felt embarrassed by that because she knew her friends knew when it was time for her to go home.

"Now, you can go to practice tomorrow, but you still can't have any phone calls." Her mother said. Inside she was happy, but of course she didn't express it on the outside. However, she wasn't too thrilled about the no phone calls part because she couldn't stand it when her mom would tell her friends she couldn't have any phone calls. How embarrassing was that? When she would go to school the next day, all she would hear was, *What did you do, I called last night and someone said you couldn't have phone calls.* That was a pet peeve for her. Obviously if that's what her mother said, then that's what it was, don't rub it in; so she didn't like when anyone questioned it, therefore she would ignore it since she didn't have a reasonable answer anyway.

Her freshman year went smooth. She didn't do too bad academically. She received honors and honorable mention awards throughout her first year. Her good academics made her mother ease off her a little also. Athletically wasn't bad for her either. The girls' basketball team won the state championship. For their remarkable effort, Lani received a team embroidered sports jacket and a ring with her name, jersey number, position and year on it. The team also received a plaque with everyone's name and the team picture on it. Not bad for a freshman, she felt like a star. After the team won the championship, however, Lani didn't want to play anymore because she felt like she got everything she wanted out of the team. She felt there wasn't any reason to continue playing since she was apart of the winning team and received a trophy. Therefore, she ended her basketball "career."

During the basketball season, Lani gained weight. When she entered high school, she was a mere one hundred pounds, and after the season, she jumped to a hundred twenty pounds. Though she looked nice and healthy because she was evenly toned with a little weight on her, she felt fat. Her mother and other people would often tell her she had a nice shape, especially since she had nice size butt, but she didn't like the weight so she didn't eat much to lose the weight.

Lani's mother dressed Lani up until junior year in high school. She dressed her like a female with nice skirts and shoes, like a young lady should be. She kept decent clothes and received many compliments, but she didn't like wearing girl clothes. Lani even had jewelry. Her mother brought her Cuban link chains, nice earrings, bracelets, ankle bracelets; she even had her wearing toe rings. She liked the jewelry, which she would often lose and be disciplined for, but she was not feeling the girl clothes; it did not make her comfortable. There were even times when she would leave her house wearing what her mother picked out for her and then change right before she got to school; and then change again once she left school and got home so her mother wouldn't know. She felt more comfortable wearing casual clothes and that's what she was going to wear regardless of what anyone thought.

It was now spring time. Lani had met a nice girl who was in most of her classes. In no time, LaReasha Jones, or Reasha for short, and Lani became tight. It wasn't clear as to how they clicked so soon, but they were always together. Lani spent most of the time at Reasha's house, which was within walking distance of her house. Reasha was different from Lani though. Reasha was sneaky on the low; she was also a gold-digger. She felt like every dude she talked to had to buy her a pair of sneakers, but of course them buying her sneakers meant they were tapping that ass too. Lani on the other hand wasn't into receiving material things from men. She carried her mother's words on her arm – "you don't need no guy to do nothing for you, that's what you got a mother for." She knew what that would lead to – nothing is for free. When a guy spends money on a chick, he definitely want some ass in return, maybe not right then and there, but you better believe eventually those panties are dropping. Like Biggie and R. Kelly proclaimed, "you must be used to me spending...and all that sweet wining and dining...but I'm fucking you tonight;" and that's exactly how every guy felt and still feel to this day.

Reasha was a bad influence on Lani. Once Lani met Reasha, she began smoking marijuana. When she first tried it, it was rolled in notebook paper. Lani didn't know how to inhale the weed though, and she didn't get high the first few times she tried it, so she pretended to be high. She knew some signs to look for in a high person, so she used that same thing to pretend. She was acting silly and laughing at everything. When she wasn't around Reasha though, she acted her regular self. Every morning she and Reasha would gather to smoke before school. One day Reasha invited a girl named Manny to smoke with them. Manny was a professional smoker and she was younger than Lani and Reasha. Lani attended elementary school with her so she knew her and didn't mind smoking with her.

Again, they rolled the weed in notebook paper because neither of them had a Dutch and they didn't have time to get one. They were out in the open with it too, smoking while walking down a main road. In the morning before school, adults rode the area on their way to work so any one of Lee's friends could have seen Lani smoking and reported that. That would be her ass if that happened but that was something she didn't think about.

While they were smoking, Manny noticed that Lani was inhaling the weed wrong. "Gimme that, you wasting the weed girl. You inhale like this." She showed Lani to inhale by sucking herself in. Like a sound you would make if you were experiencing minor pain or making a hissing sound backwards. "Try it now." She did just that and within an instant she began coughing so hard, tears were coming down her face. "That's how you do it," Manny said while she and Reasha laughed. She took two more puffs and still coughed. Her virgin lungs weren't used to smoke. By the time the weed rotated back to her, she was feeling it. She took a couple more puffs and was done. Her heart was beating extra fast, she couldn't feel herself inside her own body. She felt weird. She couldn't pretend now, she was high. When she walked, she couldn't even feel that; it felt like she could hear it though. She couldn't even speak. At this point, she didn't want to go to school. She didn't want to feel that way, and she didn't want her teachers and peers to know she was high. When she walked into school, she couldn't even act normal, and she definitely couldn't hide her bloodshot red eyes. She felt even crazier because it seemed as if everyone was staring at her, and they knew she wasn't her regular self. She couldn't do anything but sit there looking stupid, high, mouth all dry, imagination running wild and heart still pounding.

Once her first period class was over, she rushed to find Reasha. When she found her, she was so happy. "We have to go home. I feel crazy." Lani explained.

"You feel crazy, I feel blazin." Reasha replied. Of course she felt blazin, she had weed for breakfast everyday. Lani was new to this. She was an amateur and one thing she did not know was that amateurs do not fuck with professional smokers. "You wanna go to my house, nobody home."

"Yeah, come on." They left school and walked to Reasha's house. Again they both were on thin ice, especially Lani. Not only did they have to worry about parents and friends of their parents seeing them skipping school, but also undercover cops who patrolled the area for students skipping between the hours of 8 a.m. and 12 p.m.. They arrived safely though. Lani was relieved to be out of the public. She felt so safe now. She just relaxed and kept telling Reasha she wasn't ever smoking again. They ate their high away and Lani made it home about an hour after school was over.

Her high was completely down and she hoped no one saw her skipping school, nor did any teachers call her mom and tell her she skipped school. She did indeed get away with it. She was now officially addicted to getting high and skipping school. That was the last time smoking according to her – BULLSHIT! There was much more than smoking in store for her fooling around with Reasha. She turned into an addict after that.

Every morning she and a bunch of other kids would stand at the corner store, which was across the street from the school, and smoke. That gave her a good enough reason to want to get up at 6:30 a.m. for school. This was a regular routine for many students; so regular and normal that many people knew to arrive extra early to find who had the weed, roll it and get the session started. No one even cared when the principal put a camera that could see activity going on at the store; they just moved further down out of view of it. Lani would go to school stoned. Eventually regular weed didn't do anything for her anymore and she moved on to stronger quality weed like brown, hydro, chronic, and haze.

She didn't even stop smoking when she thought a male friend of hers gave her "wet." He gave her chronic, which was stronger than what she had been smoking, but that only made her want to smoke more. After that though, she vowed to never smoke with anyone unless she watched them roll it. She became weed educated and even learned to roll the weed. She kept her mind in the books despite her excessive weed smoking because she did not need her mother on her back about school. She enjoyed smoking weed and the feeling it gave her and it also made her lose some weight too – which was something she wanted to do; but she had no idea on the impact it was having on her life.

Chapter Three: The Very First Time

It was now a couple weeks before the ending of freshman year. Along with Reasha, Lani also began hanging with another female. Zanie played basketball with Lani, but she also attended the same middle school as Reasha, so Zanie and Reasha had a more stable friendship than did Reasha and Lani. One day, Zanie and Lani decided to skip school because Reasha didn't come to school. They wanted to pop up on Reasha at her house. Upon arriving at her house, they knocked on the door about twenty times. They knew she was home so they weren't about to leave after walking all the way over there, besides, where else were they going to go? After about three minutes of non-stop doorbell ringing, Reasha finally answered.

"Girl, I know you weren't sleep that hard." Lani expressed with deep anger.

"No, I have company. I thought ya'll would get the hint, I guess not." Reasha replied.

"You should have told us, we wasn't about to leave after walking all the way here." Lani retorted. There was a brief pause. "Uh...are you going to let us in or what?" Reasha didn't want to let them in because they fucked up her whole shit and she couldn't help but wonder why they were being so inconsiderate of her needs. Lani and Zanie knew they weren't wanted, but they didn't care either. They knew Reasha wouldn't be mad forever. When they walked into

25

Reasha's room, they found her boyfriend sitting on her bed looking dumbfounded. They both looked as if they were up to something.

Eventually they all became comfortable with each other and laughed at some jokes and played some games. Lani and Zanie left around their usual time – ten minutes after school was dismissed so their parents (or at least Lani's) would think they went to school. Ladell, Reasha's boyfriend, left with them. Later that night, when Reasha and Lani got on the phone, Lani couldn't help but ask what she and Radell were doing. "Sooo, what happened with you two?" Lani asked.

"What do you mean what happened?" Reasha responded.

"I'm saying, we walk in, Radell on the bed looking cheap, you came to the door in a t-shirt, what's good?"

"We was just chillin,' talkin' that's all."

"Ya'll ever did it?"

"Yeah, we did." Reasha said laughing.

"Are you serious? So you not a virgin?" Lani said shocked.

"No, today was our second time."

"Oh my god! How was it?"

"It was alright." She said laughing.

"Well did it hurt?"

"Hell yeah it hurt girl."

"The second time was bad too?"

"No, not really. At least not like the first time."

"Did he pop your cherry?"

"Yeah, the first time."

"Were you scared the first time?"

"Well kind of. It wasn't as bad as I thought it would be though. I'm sure there's worse pain than that out there."

26

"You grownnnn." Lani couldn't help her curiosity about sex. She was still a virgin, but she wanted to feel that pain. She was already involved with a boy whom she played with as a youngster. They had puppy love in elementary school and Lani never really got over him (as if there was anything to get over) and somehow they sparked that flame again.

Derek was definitely Lani's type. He was a dark chocolate young boy, with smooth skin and a smooth swagger. The relationship they resumed wasn't serious though. So Lani began talking to someone else, while still keeping in contact with Derek. The dude she began talking to also played basketball with Derek. Mike had a big crush on Lani. Mike was cute, but he was corney. He was one of those guys you would talk to on the low and if anyone ever asked about the two of you, you would definitely deny it, while he's running around claiming you. They didn't attend the same school though, that was the good thing – no one would see them together.

Lani was talking to Derek and Mike simultaneously. She was a little player and she didn't care. Lani's mother was working third shift at this time, 11 p.m. – 7 a.m. and that was sweet to Lani. One night she invited Mike over and he was more excited about the meeting than her. They relaxed, played a few games and kissed a little. He made Lani laugh and she actually enjoyed his company more than she thought she would. Although he did try, they didn't have sex.

She invited him over the next night also. Upon his arrival, he asked her if she was Derek's girlfriend. She told him no, but wondered why he had asked that. Besides, she wasn't Derek's girlfriend because they never confirmed that, or at least not to her knowledge, and she didn't belong to Mike either for that matter.

"I saw him at the gym tonight. We were talking and I asked him if he knew you..." *Why in the hell is he asking people about me, it is not that serious. He need to keep this on the low or there will be no more of this.* Lani thought to herself while listening to Mike. "He was saying yeah or whatever and how you was his girl, so I told him I talk to you on the phone and he asked me what your phone number was." Lani was upset because first of all, if Derek and her were an item, why in the world would Mike tell him they talked on the phone. She thought guys didn't do that, only females. Secondly, what type of relationship did she and Derek have if he had to ask someone else for her phone number; and he only asked for it because another dude had interest in her. That was a typical guy move anyway. A dude only shows interest in a female when there's another dude showing more interest.

"Well I don't know why he would say I'm his girlfriend if he doesn't even have my phone number." Lani replied with anger and curiosity mixed. They resumed their night. Ten minutes into his stay, the phone rung. Lani ran into the other room to get the phone. She recognized the number, it was Derek – of course she had his number. She hesitated, not wanting to answer. He was only calling because of what happened and he probably didn't know she knew what was going on, so she picked up to see what he had to say.

"What's up baby." He said with confidence as if she was really his baby, not realizing Mike was in the next room. Deep down inside she liked Derek more than Mike and she had no problem claiming Derek but she didn't like how he was trying to play her. She exhaled and sucked her teeth, *the nerve of him to call me baby,* she thought.

"Who is this?" She replied knowing damn well she knew who she was talking to.

28

"Oh now you don't know my voice?"

"No I don't obviously if I'm asking, now tell me who you are before I introduce you to my sister Toni (the dial tone)."

"Derek."

"Oh... hi." Lani responded in a brief, uninterested tone. "What made you want to call me?"

"I was thinking about you. I can't call you?"

"You don't usually call me, what's so different now?"

"Nothing...I just really wanted to talk to you for some reason, how are you?"

"I'm fine. You only called me cause you saw Mike. You didn't even have my number so what type of shit is that?" Derek was speechless. He was shocked because he didn't expect that.

"I had your number. I just didn't know it off the top of my head."

"Well I guess I'm not that important then if you can't remember my number."

"That's not true, I was trying to come see you tonight if that's possible."

"Uh, pa leeze. Stay right where you at and do what you were going to do before you saw Mike because you wasn't thinking about me." Derek lived only two blocks from Lani. She didn't want him to pop up because that would just be drama she didn't need and it just wouldn't look right.

"Okay, I see you have an attitude right now. I'll catch you on the rebound." Lani slammed the phone down. That was rude of him; she didn't like that at all. He tried to play her for a fool. Although Lani was only fourteen at the time, she was very smart, academically and street-wise, and she was also mature for her age. She was a big thinker so she always thought outside the norm. What someone else

29

thought wasn't possible, she thought of the possibility, so him playing her was not going to happen; little did he know, she was the one doing the playing.

　　She returned to her company, not mentioning the phone call she received. They continued their evening. She was feeling Mike a little more since their rendezvous, but not enough to flaunt him in public. He was a nice guy, definitely the opposite of Derek. He was light-skinned, which was not her type. She wasn't into light-skinned men for two reasons. For one, she was light-skinned so she felt she would look better with a dark-skinned man and their baby would come out with a nice caramel complexion. That was just the way she thought. She shouldn't have been thinking about any baby for that matter at her age, but she just thought hypothetically for future relationships. That was just her theory. Secondly, her father was light-skinned so she figured every light-skinned man was just like her father, which indeed was a stereotype, but that was what he instilled in her from him not being around. Despite the events that occurred with Derek, she still felt she would rather be with him than Mike.

　　When she went to school the next day, she saw Derek. He just stared at her as she walked down the hall. She glanced at him one time but kept her eyes straight ahead walking right by him without acknowledgment.

　　"You just gonna walk by me like that?" He said. She turned and responded.

　　"Like what, you didn't say nothing to me." He began walking towards her.

　　"Why I always have to say something to you?"

　　"Cause you don't. You don't call me, I'm always calling you. I know your number by heart." He smirked at her and replied.

"I called you. I just be busy that's all, that's why I don't call you as often as I should." She knew that was bullshit, like all the other lines he said to her. Maybe it would work on someone else, but Lani was far more advanced than him and any other female in her age group for that matter. "So, can I come see you tonight?" She hesitated, wondering what she should say. He just looked at her waiting for an answer, while giving her a very seductive look – a look you just couldn't say no to.

"Yeah, you can come, call me when you're on your way." What a sucker. She was supposed to make him suffer, but there was just something about him that made her want him even more. That night he did show up at her house. They talked for a while and laughed at a few memories they had together. Of course he pulled the wrestling move on her (something boys did often as a good way to get their girls into a fucking position without abruptly going for the pussy) but she kept pushing him off, until finally she gave in. As soon as she gave in, it began pouring raining outside so hard you would have thought that was God's warning to her not to do it. Warning or not, she didn't listen.

They got naked and both were ready. He was more ready than her though. He prepared to stick his dick in her virgin pussy when she stopped him. She reached on the floor to grab a condom she had ready before he even arrived as if she was prepared to fuck him, and handed it to him. He thought he was bonin' her raw – yeah right! No one should believe a man who tells a woman (ESPECIALLY A VIRGIN WOMAN) that he is going to pull out. That pussy would be so tight on his dick and feeling so good, he ain't stoppin' NUTTIN' – literally. She damn sure wasn't trying to get pregnant either for her own sake and Lee would definitely kill her. Lee made the mistake of having Lani at fifteen and she didn't want

31

her to make the same mistake. Besides, that would be a waste.
Who the hell wants to get pregnant the first time they have sex?
That would make any female not want to have sex ever again. I
guess you could say that would be the most painful first time ever.

For some reason, Derek must have been turned off after she
tried to hand him the condom because he told her he was leaving.
He said the rain was coming down and he didn't want to get caught
in it. She knew he was upset though. Maybe the rain was the
reason but at the same time, had she not stopped him, he would
have entered her and not had a care in the world about the rain. To
her, that was a sign. Maybe it wasn't meant for them to have sex, at
least not that night, so he left but they had some unfinished business
for the next time they met up.

The next night was the same thing, she had company once
again. She was becoming too comfortable with her mother working
third shift. This time it wasn't Derek coming to finish what he started,
it was Mike again. She was a little nervous because she thought
Derek would pop up at her house and knock on her bedroom window
to finish what they started the night before. She didn't want to get
caught out like that. What a story that would be at school. She had
a ninety-eight percent doubt that he would even do it, but he wasn't
too bright either. She left that thought alone and pursued other
thoughts like *what if Big Lee came home early*. Mike would definitely
be out the window faster than she could close the front door, and she
wouldn't even care how he got home. That was more important than
anything, but she didn't want to think about that embarrassment
anyway, so she continued enjoying her evening with Mike.

Somewhere in the night she found herself on top of him
kissing him. He quietly and smoothly got her clothes off. He kissed
her all over and even sucked on her petite titties. He was definitely

excited and confidently pulled his pants off. She never had sex before, so she really couldn't distinguish between a big dick and a small one, but when she saw Mike's, she didn't even think he would reach her hyman tissue (technical name for the tissue that breaks during penetration, known as cherry popping). She wondered if dicks were supposed to be that size, but she didn't know any better; Derek was a little bigger than Mike, but he wasn't that big either, so she thought that was standard. His dick was so small, she could have probably put two fingers in her pussy and gotten the same effect; but she did give him the pussy, resulting in him being her "first."

The pain she felt made her so happy that Mike did have a "baby dick" because had it been the average size, she probably would not have been able to take it. Every thrust felt as though someone was stabbing her with a knife in her uterus. Luckily he didn't last long either, about three minutes, but he did last long enough to pop her cherry. When they were done, there was blood on the sheets. She felt awkward and didn't have anything to say. What were they to talk about now? What were they to say? She didn't want him to ask her how it was because that would have turned her off completely, and she didn't want to talk about what happened anyway. She just wanted him to leave at that point. Of course he didn't want to. He rolled over and cuddled with her. He couldn't wait to get back to the world and run his mouth about what happened (like he really did something) and Lani knew he would. She damn sure wasn't going to admit it though.

The next day at school, Lani didn't even tell Reasha what happened. She kind of had regrets about what happened because he wasn't even the one she wanted to give her virginity to, but being that she was rushing to experience sex (which could have waited because it wasn't all it was cracked up to be, she gave it to anybody.

33

She kept it to herself though. When she saw Derek she felt bad because she knew eventually they would finish what they started and she didn't want him to notice she wasn't a virgin anymore. She knew he wanted to be the one to take her virginitiy. For some reason, probably egotistical, a man feels good when he takes a females' virginity.

"What's up? Why you didn't call me last night?" He asked.

"Here you go with that again, why I didn't call you? You know my number, or do you have to get it from someone?"

"You funny." He said laughing. "No, I actually did call you last night."

"When, what time?" She asked curiously because she had caller ID and her phone didn't rang all night so she couldn't wait to hear his response.

"About 11 o'clock."

"Yeah Derek? Eleven o'clock huh? That's funny cause I didn't see your number on that little thing they invented called caller ID that lets you see the phone number of the people who called you for the day." Lani began to think maybe it was meant for her and Mike to have sex because everything coordinated perfectly, no interruptions. The night prior to that with Derek was just a disaster.

"I was just going to pop up but I didn't know if your mother was home or what." He replied. Lani stopped any other words he was thinking about saying and let him have it.

"Don't ever pop up at my house. That is so disrespectful." Lani said immediately all humor completely gone. That was her answer but she couldn't help but to imagine what would have happened had Derek knocked on her window, especially if her and Mike were having sex at that moment. She didn't know if that was worse or if he had knocked on the window while Lee was home and in her room. Derek just laughed at her. He loved how feisty she was. He couldn't understand how someone so small had such a powerful mouth.

"So can I come see you tonight?"

"Fine. Call me. If you don't call me, I'm not calling you. We'll see how bad you want to come see me." Of course he would call, any guy would when there's pussy involved and especially pussy he never had before. So of course he did call. She wasn't going to answer but she did want to see him. She just hoped if anything went down, he wouldn't notice she just fucked somebody the night before. Like he would care anyway, but he would probably be mad if someone other than him took her virginity.

When he arrived it felt like deja vu. There was a guy with her every night. At least it was only two different guys and not one for every day of the week. She didn't care anyway. She was young and having fun. She didn't belong to any of the guys. Maybe they were claiming her but she wasn't claiming them. She was basically playing the man's game. Why couldn't she, men do it. There isn't any difference between a man and a woman except genitals, fuck that double standard bullshit. A woman should just have more respect for herself – bottom line. The problem is, men and women run their mouths about what they do behind closed doors and make it seem worse than what it really is. Damn, what ever happened to "every little thing that we do should be between me and you?"

"What's up Lani?" Derek said. She loved when he said her name. He always said it in a cute way.

"What's good?" He kissed her on her cheek and walked to her room. They sat on the bed, she laid down and he stayed sitting upright. They were quiet for about ten minutes, flicking through channels. They both wondered who would be the icebreaker.

35

"So what's up with you and Lisa?" Lani asked inquisitively. Lisa was a girl who went to the same school as them. She was black and white mixed, very skinny with extra big lips. She favored the singer Mya. She wasn't the ugliest girl, but she wasn't the prettiest either. She and Lani talked because they shared some classes together. The two of them even knew they both were involved with Derek but obviously they didn't mind.

"What's up with us?" Derek replied smiling.

"You fuck with her right?"

"No." No was his answer because he didn't fuck with her, he just fucked her whenever. He basically just dissed her and she was crazy in love with him, but he did not feel the same way about her at the time – or so he said.

"Yeah whatever, she don't act crazy over you for nothing. I don't care anyway." Lani really did care though. She liked Derek and although she was doing her thing, she didn't want anyone else to have him. Derek just laughed and started playing with her. You know what that usually mean, something was about to go down. Touching eventually led to kissing and Derek between her legs. He slowly took her pants off and his too. This time he was prepared, he brought a condom of his own and put it on. He didn't stick it in right away he just kept kissing her, giving her mini four play, as if he knew what he was doing. They were both young and did not know what they were doing when it came to sex, no matter how much they thought they knew about it. He finally went to put it in, or at least he thought he did. He was moving in and out, but he wasn't inside her. She couldn't understand how he thought he was; was it the first time for him or what? He kept it going too. *I hope this nigga not serious, this better be a part of his foreplay,* she thought; but he was serious. She pretended right along with him, moaning and screaming like it

36

hurt. Some way, somehow he came. He came quick too, like three minutes; which always feel like an eternity when you're faking it. She was glad it was over though.

When it was all said and done, he rolled over and went to sleep. Lani was livid. Ironically, she was thinking about Mike and what he was doing. She didn't even get to feel what Derek was like. He couldn't even find the hole, what a cornball, and what a waste of time. After ten minutes, he woke up and told Lani he was leaving. He kissed her and told her he was going to call her tomorrow. She was glad he was leaving. She didn't even say bye to him and she didn't want him calling either.

The next day at school, Lani had hickees on her neck that she didn't even know she had. Her mother didn't see them on her neck, but she showed them off in school to let everyone know she too, was sexually active (which always seems "cool" in high school). Reasha noticed and couldn't help but point it out. She told her Derek put them there when Mike was really the one who put the hickees on her. It was dark when Derek saw her the night before, so he didn't see the hickees either. She told Reasha she lost her virginity to Derek and when Reasha saw Derek, she laughed and asked him why he put the hickees on Lani's neck.

"I didn't mean to do that." He said confusingly. His dumb ass didn't even know he didn't put hickees on someone's neck. He couldn't find a hole and he couldn't find a clue. No wonder he was in low level classes (and he really was). At this point, she was convinced it was not meant for them to have sex. It didn't happen the first time because Mother Nature didn't allow it and the second time he just didn't know what he was doing. The way she felt, if it was meant to be, it would happen eventually – when it was destined to happen.

37

Chapter Four: THE CLOSEST – MOST GRIMY

Lani was now a sophomore. She survived her freshman year, which was a very interesting one. She smoked weed for the first time and had sex for the first time, she was basically being a follower. She smoked because Reasha did it and she had sex because Reasha did it – peer pressure is a bitch. On the other side of town though, Marie was doing the same thing. She had a homegirl she was cool with who turned her out on weed and she had already experienced sex.   Her first experience was special though. She did it with her boyfriend who she was with since sixth grade. After giving up her fear of kissing, because her mother warned her at an early age that if she kissed a boy she would get pregnant (she really believed that and she really didn't kiss her boyfriend until high school), she finally gave herself to him. It was his first time also, which made it so special. Though she had a cute relationship, she was young and in an abusive one. She had a Puerto Rican boyfriend who treated her good for their age, but he often would beat on her, and even broke her finger at one point in their relationship. Though her family didn't like him because of that, she still stayed with him because she "loved" him, and eventually she got pregnant by him and later aborted the baby.

Around this time, Marie and Nisha were coming back into Lani's life. Their clique was evolving. It consisted of Lani, Marie, Nisha, Reasha, Zani, and Marie's cousin Roni. Marie came to the school everyday afterschool to hang with them. She didn't really

38

know Zani or Reasha like that. Every morning before school, everyone except Marie, followed their daily routine which was smoking at the corner store. Lani began paying more attention to Nisha and Marie at this time. She was cool with Reasha and Zani, but she had been cool with Nisha and Marie since middle school. Reasha was off the hook anyway. All she wanted to do was smoke all day and she started messing with a bunch of dudes. She was fucking different dudes for money, weed, whatever. She wasn't fucking with ballers though, she was fucking with regular ass niggas. She may have gotten a few dollars here and there, maybe some weed, or maybe a pair of sneakers too, but nothing major. She was just loose. So Lani started hanging with Nisha and Marie on a regular basis.

Lani sensed a change in Reasha, but she never really paid any attention to it. She had no idea Reasha was jealous of the relationship she shared with Nisha and Marie. They were all cool though and they smoked together whenever possible, so she had no idea there was a hidden tension. But with the majority of situations, just because you get high with someone, doesn't make them your peoples.

Lani became involved with a boy who went to the same school as Marie. He was actually friends with Marie and at one point it was rumored they were fucking each other. That was a lie though, that was just the type of person Mauri was. He was a hoe, and he wasn't even all that attractive. He was getting a little money and he was known to trick a little. That wasn't the reason Lani began talking to him though. It was just something about him, probably because at the time he was just the "it" nigga and he liked her first. She didn't care about what a dude had in his pocket, just him being well groomed and neat in appearance was enough for her; a dude could have a fresh pair of white Uptowns or a pair of "crispy" Tims and he was good with her. She was never looking for anything serious with Mauri and neither was he, they were just fucking partners, as any other female he had was.

Lani knew she had other brothers and sisters on her father side, but she never knew who they were. From the brief moment her father came in her life (as he often did) when she was in junior high, she was introduced to her brother, who also went to the same school and they didn't know. That wasn't good at all because what if they would have gotten involved with one another not even knowing they were related. They did look alike too. Lani also heard her father mention that he had another daughter about a year older than Lani, named Percenna who he thought wasn't his child (as he did with Lani until she got older and looked like him). Lani remembered the name and one day in math class she was chatting with one of her classmates who happened to be named Percenna. Lani didn't think anything of it because she was brown-skinned and all his other children were light-skinned, until she stated she didn't really have her father in her life. That statement made Lani think about what her name was and asked her who her father was. She and Lani did have the same father and Lani met her older sister. Though they knew they were sisters, it was too late in the game to embrace one another since they didn't know each other. They established their roots, but that was about it, at least they knew who each other were which was more important than anything; no matter what, a child should always know their family members.

Lani and Reasha were still tight. In fact, when Lani and Mauri got up for the first time, Reasha let Lani use her house while her parents were at work. Coincidentally, Mauri was Reasha's ex-boyfriend's (Radell) cousin. Lani had Mauri thinking it was her house

40

they were creeping at and they fucked right on Reasha's bed. Of course Lani never told Reasha that because that's something you just don't do, but if it was vice versa, Reasha would have done the same thing. They left before school was out and Lani returned back to school around dismissal time. She encountered Reasha talking to a guy named Lamar. Lani heard some things about Lamar but she was young so she never took heed to it.

Lamar was about three years older than them. He was tall, light-skinned, and very handsome (actually blazin), and he was getting money – definitely Reasha's type. However, it was rumored he was the police (local snitch), and that he had AIDS. Lani would later confirm what she heard when her cousin began getting money with him. The two men took a trip to New York to purchase some blow. Lani's cousin had a gun on him to protect him from the ruthless vultures in New York and they were pulled over. Lamar told authorities the gun belonged to Lani's cousin and he was charged with gun possession. In fact, his nickname was "Grimy." They said that according to him, he didn't use a condom with any girl he fucked. Obviously no one cared about this or took it seriously because he still had bitches on his dick. Reasha exchanged numbers with him and she was happy because she thought she was something special, not realizing she was just another girl who he was about to fuck – with no condom according to him. If Lani wasn't smarter than Reasha, she definitely had enough sense. She didn't care how fine a guy was, no guy was worth dying over. All it took was one time for her to hear someone had AIDS and that was enough, regardless of how blazin he was and whether true or not, she wasn't risking it.

It was about two weeks since Reasha began talking to Lamar. She had Lani and Nisha thinking she was just going to get a pair of sneakers out of him and that would be that; she wanted to show

41

them just how tight her game was. She had them under the impression that her pussy was so blazin that she didn't have to ask for shit, niggas just threw money at her. So when Lani and Nisha saw Reasha they wanted to know which sneakers he got her.

"What's up? You got those?" Nisha asked her, the three of them standing in front of Reasha's locker.

"Got what?"

"Them kicks from Lamar?"

"Nah, he a wrap, I don't even talk to him anymore." Reasha responded.

"Why what happened?" Lani questioned.

"I don't know, we just stopped talking. I guess we didn't have good chemistry."

"So damn, you didn't even get a pair of kicks? You cheap." Nisha said jokingly, she and Lani laughing. Reasha didn't find that funny though, she was insulted.

"I ain't cheap, fuck ya'll bitches." She replied seriously and walked away. Lani and Nisha just looked at each other wondering what the anger was about. Was she mad that she fucked him and didn't get what she was supposed to out the deal? She never admitted that she fucked Lamar, but it was kind of obvious. Reasha took Nisha's joke to heart and she didn't like how Lani laughed at the joke. Lani had no idea Reasha had revenge on her mind for something so silly. Maybe that wasn't the real reason; it may have been an excuse because deep down inside Reasha thought Lani was trying to dis her for Nisha and Marie.

Lani was still talking to Mauri at this time and she went to his house often. He lived in the projects called the "G," short for the "Ghetto." They talked on the phone here and there, but they basically had a sexual relationship. Lani didn't know why she was

42

fucking Mauri, she didn't find him attractive like that and he had exzema around his mouth. She was just open that's all, and not on him, on dick; and dick was dick to her, it was all the same once she got her shit off. After a while though, she just said fuck him, he wasn't worth her time and coincidently he felt the same way. They eventually cut ties with each other.

It was now the end of sophomore year. Reasha still wasn't really fucking with Lani like that. They were tight in the past with an unbreakable bond, but somewhere, somehow, their relationship deteriorated. Reasha was still hoeing, nothing changed about that. She was in every nigga's face like it was nothing, still fucking for weed and money. She did get a couple niggas who brought her an outfit, maybe a pair of sneakers, but of course she returned the favor. She was loose. That was one of the reasons Lani fell back from her. She loved Reasha though; she felt so close to her. They did a lot together and all of a sudden they weren't so close anymore. They still did things together and talked to each other, but they were each into their own thing. As you get older, people change, love changes, nothing stays the same, no matter how much you would like it to. Lani had more freedom than she did previously, but somehow she found a way to abuse her freedom. Lani wasn't a bad kid, she was just a follower. The summer after her sophomore year was crazy because she was on punishment the whole summer. For some odd reason, Lani felt the need to steal a pizza delivery vehicle. One nice summer day, Lani, Nisha, and Zanie were hanging out at Nisha's house. Lani and Nisha tried on prior attempts to steal a pizza delivery car, but were unsuccessful due to their inexperience with driving. So this day they decided to try again. They called a pizza delivery to an address that was just two blocks from Lani's home. They rode two bikes to the destination and waited for the delivery man to arrive. Lani would be the driver so she handed her bike over to Zanie and told them to meet her around the corner as they waited anxiously to see what would happen.

When the pizza man arrived and went up the stairs to the house he was delivering to, Lani jumped in the car and threw the gears in reverse to back up because the car was a bit close to a parked car. The delivery man heard the car, turned around and began chasing the car. Panicked by the man, Lani continued pressing on the gas while still in reverse. She backed into a parked van and damaged both vehicles. She still tried to get away, still not realizing the car was in reverse as the cars were sustaining more damage. After realizing she wouldn't be able to get away in the car, she threw the gears in the park position and got out the car and began running. Nisha and Zanie looked on in amazement. She ran about two blocks down the street toward her house, spectators watching and all. She was out of breath and decided to hide on the side of a house, which was diagonally across the street from her house and in plain view of her mother's window. She thought she had gotten away until some nosey spectators told the delivery man where she was. She was caught and the police were called.

Lani's mother had no idea what was going on right outside her bedroom until a neighbor knocked on her door and told her. Lee was furious and she went outside to scold her daughter. She was also crying because she just did not know what the fuck her daughter was thinking. That wasn't like Lani and she knew there had to be other people involved who influenced her decision. Both Lee and the police questioned Lani about the involvement of other people so they could be punished too, but Lani took the sole responsibility of her actions and did not snitch on Zanie and Nisha.

She was taken to the precinct, fingerprinted, and released that night on a promise to appear (PTA). Her mother put her on punishment for the whole summer. She was on punishment with no phone privileges and couldn't go outside. Her phone privileges came back gradually, but she really was not able to go outside until two weeks before summer was over. Lee convinced the prosecutor that Lani's behavior was not like her and she brought report cards to show what a good student she was. The charges were thrown out only if she completed forty hours of community service within a given time period – in which she did.

Going into junior year was no different from the previous two years. Lani was smoking more than ever by this time. Shockingly, it didn't affect her in school. Although she got high every morning, she had her best academic year in high school. Her smoking was bad though. Not only did she smoke every morning, but she even smoked at home – while her mother was there. She would go in the back hallway of her home when her mother was sleep or into a phone conversation when she knew she wasn't getting up any time soon. When she was finished smoking, she would wash her face, neck, and hands with soap (since that was where most of the smoke resided) and change her shirt just in case her mother did get up and possibly decided to talk to her. Another way she would get her smoke on would be in her room, with her door closed, smoking out of her window and then lit incense afterwards. She would only smoke this way once Lee was asleep. She would smoke twice a day at the minimum, which was more than she ever planned to.

She was now tighter than ever with Nisha and Marie. They would skip school and go to Nisha's house and chill, get high and laugh at shit. Most of the time though, Nisha and Lani would just be waiting on Marie; because instead of skipping school and going to Nisha's house like she was supposed to, she would go to her boyfriend's house. Nisha and Lani would get so mad at her because Marie was no longer with her first "love," she was with a new kid named Torey. She ended her first relationship when she met Torey because she was so attracted to his looks. She loved her first love and she may have stayed with him if she hadn't heard he was cheating. Torey was no better though. Marie caught him cheating on numerous occasions, but she still stayed with him. There were even times he was seen by the three of them with another chick. This was the reason Marie and Lani would get upset because Marie would dis them to be with Torey even at times when he was caught cheating two hours prior. She wouldn't take any actions against him. Instead, she would cry to Lani and Nisha, tell them she was straight on him with his "little ass dick," and then be right back in the bed with him. But Lani and Nisha didn't understand at the time that love and emotions is a powerful thing.

No matter how many times Nisha and Lani would tell her to leave him, it was useless because everything went in one ear and out the other. Shit, Lani was glad it wasn't her, because she was involved with Torey when she was in the eighth grade but it was just puppy love, nothing happened and that was that. Since Lani and Marie weren't in touch with each other around that time and their relations happened when they were young, it was nothing. Torey also had an older sister who was a psycho bitch. Tracey was grimy and phony and like her brother, she couldn't be trusted. She would tell Marie when her brother was cheating, and Torey never knew. She was also a baby making machine, fertile as ever. A dude could probably impregnate her through the condom.

46

Nisha had a smart mouth when it came to Marie and Torey's situation, always being sarcastic. She didn't mean anything by it, that was just who she was. She was a virgin up to junior year in high school. She would always ask Lani and Marie questions about sex, she was so curious, but never got around to experiencing it. She did it the smart way – she waited.

Junior year in high school was a good year. Lani experienced the junior prom, she matured more, and she did better than ever academically. She no longer talked with Derek either, he was old news. She left him alone so he could be with Lisa, besides, he heard about Mike and a couple other dudes. Although she denied it, she didn't appreciate him calling her a hoe. Guys are crazy with that shit. They don't really want you until another guy shows interest, then they get all mad when you give up YOUR pussy that they think is theirs, but they never stop to ask themselves, *how could that be my pussy if I was neglecting it?* In his case, how was Lani's pussy his? He never felt inside it. So that was that, she didn't even speak to him when she saw him in school, she acted like he never existed.

Now remember Mauri? He was back in the picture, but this time for a different reason. Mauri tried to holla at Reasha. Reasha knew him and she also knew Mauri and Lani fucked, shit, they even fucked on Reasha's bed before. But Reasha was a straight up grimy slut bitch with not only revenge on her mind, but her best interest also. She tried to front like she didn't holla at him, when all along she was messing with him. She [Reasha] knew he had a little money and he would probably trick on her, which was her main reason for giving him the time of day. But Lani wondered if she was also getting back at her for something in the past. It wasn't clear that they were talking until Reasha showed up to school with his chain on. That was

47

something Nisha had to pull Lani out of class for and call Marie at school from the pay phone for.

"Bitch…" Nisha paused. "Why the fuck I think Reasha got Mauri chain on. I'm not sure but it looks like his. Marie said he don't have his chain on in school today."

"Are you serious, so they talk huh?" Lani asked shockingly waiting for a confirmation.

"I think so, I will try to get some info from her [Reasha] in class fifth period okay."

"Yeah you do that." Although Mauri wasn't all that attractive and he was never anybody Lani cared for, it was fucked up that Reasha would do that to her. Friends don't let niggas run through the crew, it just doesn't look right. Lani didn't know how Reasha felt, but she didn't want to be apart of a crew that niggas ran through. That showed her right there she was nothing but a hoe who would betray her friends to get something from a guy. She didn't care either. Prior to this day, she was still talking to Lani like everything was all good while she was stabbing her in the back. Lani tried to say fuck it, don't let a nigga come between their friendship but she just couldn't. It is impossible for two females who had sex with the same guy to be friends; for some men it is impossible also depending on the situation, but a lot easier than women.

To investigate the situation, Nisha wrote Reasha a letter in the class they shared together. They passed notes back and forth. Reasha confirmed she was seeing Mauri stating she didn't mean for it to happen the way it did. She claimed Mauri was persistent so she gave him her number only intending to talk to him. Somehow that turned into more. And of course it would. There's no such thing as just wanting to be friends with someone of the opposite sex, and especially someone who wanted to holla at you for that matter.

48

Nisha asked why she didn't tell Lani and asked her why she tried to hide it. Reasha told her she planned on telling Lani and that she didn't try to hide it. She had no remorse though. It was like she did it on purpose and it was as if she wanted Nisha to be the bearer of bad news.

From that point on, Reasha and Lani didn't talk. It was awkward because Lani loved Reasha like a sister. She couldn't believe she did that. She tried to forget it and just say, *you know what, he ain't worth the drama, fuck niggas don't let them come between us*, but she knew their relationship would never be the same. Lani gave it a try though; after a week she called Reasha. Their conversation went good at first but then they got into an argument. After that, Lani said *fuck it*, and it was on from then.

Chapter Five: A New Life

It was now mid summer and Lani was headed into her last year of high school. She had a wild summer and even her spring was crazy. She had the bullshit with Reasha happen and she hooked up with Derek in July after flirting with him (after not speaking to him for about six months). He came over her house one night and he finally knew what he was doing. He must have practiced since their previous two sessions that failed. He deceived Lani though. He made her think he had a condom on and really didn't so he fucked her and came in her, but she didn't know until afterwards and she was mad about it. Up until that point, she felt good about her sexual life because she was practicing safe sex.

She continued her habits, (smoking and doing whatever). One day she went out to the "G" with Marie. While hanging out with the dudes they knew out there, Mauri popped up. Lani was over the fact that Reasha shitted on her, so she moved on with her life. On the other hand though, she had revenge on her mind, but she didn't know what it would be.

"What's up Lani." Mauri said grabbing her thigh.

"Don't touch her, ain't nobody fucking with you." Marie said jokingly, but also seriously.

"Yeah, don't touch me. Go touch Reasha." Lani said.

"Man, go ahead with that. I don't fuck with her like that." Mauri said just like most grimy niggas do – never want to claim their property.

50

"Oh, please, don't do that. Claim your property. You know that's wifey. And she had on your Coogi sweatsuit in school, so she definitely your wifey." Lani replied, she and Marie laughing as they recalled the day Reasha did indeed have on his sweatsuit.

"Yeah, she sure did." Marie added with humor.

"Man I don't fuck with that girl like that. She can't even fuck, she just lay there, don't even move around. Anyway, she not my wifey, you are. What's up though? Come upstairs so I can show you something." At first Lani wasn't going to go because she was not feeling him. He was corney and he was a hoe. But she also knew what that meant, he wasn't slick at all. So she went. After he said what he said about Reasha, she knew she had to step up her game so no nigga could ever say anything like that about her. When they got upstairs, he pulled a sock out his draw that had $1800 in it. For what? Lani didn't know because he wasn't giving it to her so what was the point. That's exactly what she meant by him being corney. He was playing himself and he wasn't a baller. He did put the moves on her and she gave in. Not cause she wanted to, but because she wanted to expose him to Reasha if she ever found out. Reasha thought he would treat her differently, but she was no different than any other female he fucked with. Lani fucked him that time and another time months later. Reasha found out about both times, but believed Mauri and thought Lani was just jealous; not even realizing that Lani didn't want Mauri not one bit. The second time they fucked was in the new house he moved to in the "Hill". Reasha didn't believe Lani despite the fact Lani described things that were in his new room, including a hat in his closet that had a female's name on it, who he was dealing with in New Jersey. Reasha continued relations with him and later went on to have his baby.

51

It was now senior year, Lani survived high school; but not quite yet. Although she felt like she couldn't trust anyone, she still felt close to Nisha and Marie. Marie even transferred schools and attended the same school as Lani and Nisha. Nisha and Marie still talked with Reasha, but it was phony, as was Lani and Zanie's relationship. Lani liked Zanie still, but because she still hung with Reasha, she didn't know what to expect from her. They didn't trust them bitches, especially Reasha. And the whole time, Lani tried to tell Nisha and Marie not to talk to her because it was just a matter of time before she got them. They just used her for information though. Reasha would brag about how Mauri brought her sneakers and outfits. They would then run and tell Lani, but Lani didn't care. She wasn't mad that Reasha had Mauri because he was a nobody anyway. She was mad that her friend betrayed her but she knew karma would come back around somehow, someway. That's the way Lani looked at things. She always put revenge in God's hands because she was too kindhearted and she knew God's punishment would always be worse than any punishment she would ever give.

They should have listened when Lani tried to warn them about Reasha. One day in class Reasha, Marie, and another female were sharing secrets. Marie told Reasha about a boy she fucked. Marie fucked the boy while she was with Torey but while he was incarcerated. Torey at this time was coming off the porch, so he tried to make a name for himself in the streets; in doing that, he would be in and out of jail. The boy Marie fucked, was dealing with Manny (the girl Lani got high with her first "real" time smoking) around this time and Marie was also cool with Manny.

Reasha leaked the information out and it got back to Torey and Manny. Manny wanted to fight Marie but after they talked over their differences, Manny couldn't be mad because it was before her, but she felt Marie should have told her so she could have never become involved with him; but Marie didn't care about the boy like that, she just wanted to have sex with him. Torey was mad too. Despite all his wrongdoing, he put their business on Front Street; he wasn't about to look like a chump. He started telling people that Marie sucked his dick and she didn't know what she was doing at first but got better. Marie denied the allegations but continued a normal relationship with him. Nisha and Lani didn't find out it was true until about six years later when Marie revealed it to them during a tell-all conversation.

It had been four months since she hooked up with Derek. Lani felt a change in her body, but she didn't know exactly what. She left it alone, but she knew something was wrong. She continued her life and stayed focused in school. She started submitting her college applications and making decisions on what college she wanted to attend. She wanted to attend school for journalism since she loved to write, and could write well. She was strong academically, but she had regrets about quitting basketball after freshman year because she would have been an even better candidate with academics and athletics under her belt; even though she felt no reason to continue playing basketball because they won the championship her first year, she also quit basketball behind chasing boys and being grown. She knew if she hadn't chased boys or if they hadn't chased her, she would have stayed focused; but this was her life, these were the cards she was dealt.

She was still going to be Lani, no one could change that. There was a boy she had her eyes on who attended her school. She always saw him and thought he was cute. She finally said, *you know what, I got to have him*, and in turn told Marie she thought he was

53

blazin. Turned out, it was Marie's cousin on her father's side. Marie told Donell about Lani who was sitting by the pay phones in the lunchroom pretending she didn't know what was going on. Donell was also checking her out, so he told Marie to tell her to come to him.

"He want you girl." Marie told Lani.

"What you mean he want me?" Lani asked.

"He want to talk to you, go talk to him."

"He do? I'm scared."

"Girl, don't be scared." Lani walked over to him. She wasn't thinking though because she looked a mess. She had a big hoody on, some baggy jeans and her hair wasn't done, but this was an everyday thing for some reason. Lani always dressed like a boy, but in a cute way; but lately, she wore the same big, red hoody with a man's Avirex coat. She became lazy, and didn't want to get dressed; she was always tired, and didn't stay in school the full day. Although she looked a mess, she didn't care. The way she looked at it – she was definitely a dime if she could pull guys on her off days. So she approached him.

"What's up?" She asked.

"What's good with you." He replied with a big smile.

"Nothing, just chilling."

"So what's your name?"

"Lani, what's yours?"

"Donell. I see you was checking me out." Lani laughed when he said that. The nerve of the conceited bastard.

"Actually, No, I just thought you were cute."

"Well I was checking you out."

"Oh really?"

"Yeah really. I'm saying, the bell about to ring and I have to get out of here. So can I call you?" Donell was smooth, but he was also a player as was most guys. He was a small time hustler in the street, obsessed with sneakers and nice outfits. He had a girlfriend who he was with since he was fifteen, but that usually doesn't stop most guys. Had Lani known this though, she would have not gotten involved with him in the first place. She didn't like coming second to another girl. She wanted to be the one and only. But she gave him her number. He called about two weeks later, but by the time he called, she wasn't really interested anymore and she was aggravated by him before she even got to know him. His conversation was dry, so from that night on, she didn't answer when he called, so eventually he stopped calling.

Every morning, Lani would get up for school and put on the same hoody and maybe a shirt underneath. Lee noticed her daughter was wearing the same thing when she would arrive home from school. One morning when Lee didn't go to work, she asked Lani the question before she left.

"Are you pregnant?" Lee asked her daughter. Lani gave her a confused look like *are you serious* and replied,

"No."

"Well why haven't you been getting dressed lately? You've been wearing that same hoody. You look a mess." Lee knew how to give her daughter constructive criticism. She may have been harsh at times, but it was for her own good. She always had her daughter's best interest at heart so she would give it to her raw and uncut.

"Well it's been cold and I just wear it to school and take it off when I get there."

"When's the last time you had your period?"

"I just got over it two days ago." Lee just looked at Lani suspiciously, but she had to accept what her daughter was telling her. Lee still thought her daughter was a virgin. She was probably in denial because she wasn't dumb; she probably just didn't want to accept it. Lani was getting her period though. It was very irregular, but Lani didn't think anything of it, she just knew blood was coming out her vagina like a period so she didn't question it.

"Alright, have a good day." Lee told her daughter. Around this time, Lani's father was back in her life. He was always in and out the picture as usual, but this was the longest he had stayed around and he was actually trying to be a father. Unlike her mother who could hold grudges with anyone until her death, she forgave her father for never being there for her and taking care of her, but she hadn't forgotten. She felt if she couldn't forgive others, how would she be able to ask God for forgiveness? The relationship with her father wasn't the best father and daughter relationship, but it was better than she was used to. No matter how much Lee hated Lani's father, never once did she try to keep Lani away from her father. She wanted Lani to make her own judgment, and although Lee knew it would hurt Lani, she wanted her to see him for the coward he was. She called him occasionally and they went places, but he couldn't make up for all the time he missed. She praised him for trying though. However, just when things in her life was looking good, it took a turn for the worst; and we all know bad times can last so much longer than good times.

One evening, Lee told Lani she was stepping out. Lani knew by the way her mother was dressed whether she was taking a store trip, or a fun evening type of trip. So when her mother left, she rolled up the weed she had from earlier in the day. She went out to the back hallway like she usually did and took about three puffs. Next thing she knew, she heard footsteps coming towards her. It was Lee headed towards her room. She called Lani's name but she stayed in the hallway and didn't respond, praying Lee didn't smell the weed and open the back door. When Lee got no response, she walked back to the front of the house. Lani went back into the house and to her room. She was pissed that her mother came back as quickly as she did. She pondered what she would do and say, especially with the fresh smell of weed on her breath and body. About a minute after going back in her room, Lee headed towards the back again.

"Where were you?" Lee asked raising her voice slightly. Lani thought of an answer quickly.

"I was out back talking to Rachel." Rachel was one of the girls who lived upstairs from them.

"You smell like weed. You was smoking?"

"No." Lani said with her voice cracking. Lee began smelling Lani's hands and breath. She knew Lani was high. Lani was upset because she (after four years) got caught. Nothing was worse than getting caught while you're high. Not only was she in trouble, but her high was being messed up simultaneously. She now knew exactly how Marie felt when she was caught by her employer smoking with a co-worker on their break. The two of them were fired and since the manager was cool with Marie's mother, he called and told her about her daughter. Marie's mother picked her up at the peak of her high and scolded her. She too, couldn't enjoy her high and got in trouble.

"Yes you were. You high right now." Lee continued. Lani was speechless. There was nothing she could say, so she just kept quiet. Lee slapped her as hard as she could and Lee was heavy handed. She walked out the room and called Lani's father (whom she hated all her life). She told him about Lani and then Lee called her and told her to pick up the other phone. When Lani picked up, she was highly upset to hear her father's voice. According to Lani, he was in no position to tell her anything. For one, he recently appeared in her life; she didn't even really know him like that so to her, he was a stranger. For two, he did cocaine/crack at one time in his life and probably still did. All she did was smoke a little weed so he really was in no position to degrade her. For three, since when did Lee ever let him in on anything that went on? So when Lani talked to him, she got smart with him. She felt as if she had that right to talk to him any way she felt, besides, who the hell was he other than a sperm donor? She wanted to pull his card and tell him she saw him on the sexual offender database and how he was always trying to talk to one of her friends, so he damn sure did not want to get her started on his ass. He was accused by her brother's mother of sexual assault and therefore had to register as a sexual predator, which would follow him everywhere he went for the rest of his life.

Lee and Lani's father made her feel bad during the conversation. When all was said and done though, Lani felt the urge for more weed. She was stressed the fuck out. Her mother tried to talk to her about drugs and the effects it could have on her. She knew her daughter would ultimately make her own decision, but she wanted to make sure she had a role in her choosing the right one. Afterwards, Lee put her on punishment, something she was used to anyway. She couldn't go anywhere and couldn't use the phone. Lani thought things couldn't get any worse, but she was definitely wrong.

About two weeks later, as Lani was doing her homework, Lee called her into her room. "Lani, you pregnant?" Lee asked again.

What the fuck, you just asked me that two weeks ago and I told you the same thing. Nothings changed, she thought. "No." She replied, but she herself didn't know if she believed she wasn't. The funny thing was, about two days prior, two people asked her if she was pregnant, and weeks before that, people were asking Marie and Nisha.

"Come here, lift up your shirt." Lani lifted her shirt and looked down at her own belly. Lee felt it and said confidently, "You pregnant."

"No, I'm not."

"Look at your belly, it's round and hard." For some reason, a mother knows when their daughter is pregnant. Lani just stood there silent as usual. "You know what, I'm going to call your father and have him take us to the doctor so you can get a pregnancy test." *What the fuck is she calling him for, we don't need his ass and he don't need to be involved in this,* she thought while staring at the floor as if ashamed. Lee called her baby's daddy and they all went to the doctor. The whole ride there, Lani's father kept asking if she was pregnant and if she was having sex. Lani answered "No" to all questions. He assured her that the test would confirm whatever they wanted to know so she should come clean. But Lani kept her ground and left it at that.

At the doctor's office, Lani was nervous. She had all types of thoughts running through her head. She wasn't really sure if she was pregnant, but everyone else noticed. She received the pregnancy test and the doctor confirmed she was indeed pregnant. Lani still did not want to tell her parents even though she didn't want to keep it. When she came out the room, Lee immediately asked her if she was pregnant. She told her No, but Lee didn't believe that, so she asked the doctor. "Ma'am, we're not allowed to give that information to anyone other than the patient." The doctor said confusingly and nervously.

"This is my daughter. I have a right to know what's going on." Lee explained. After about two minutes of bickering with the doctor, Lee finally got the information she needed but did not want to know. The three of them walked out the doctor's office more furious than when they entered. Both parents seemed more distraught at the fact that Lani still lied even after the pregnancy test came back, as if they wouldn't find out the results. Lani was speechless and shocked. Her main concern wasn't what her parents thought, but rather what everyone else would think. She didn't want anyone to know but eventually people would find out, especially since Lee commanded her to call Derek and tell him.

When they arrived home, Lee was upset. She was crying and she couldn't believe her daughter was pregnant. From what she knew, her only child was a virgin. But Lee was a different parent. She was very supportive of her daughter and never turned her back on her, NO MATTER WHAT. Although she was angry, she was willing to back her daughter up one hundred percent. Lee couldn't understand why her words didn't prevent this. Time after time she warned Lani "don't be like me, finish school, get a good job, become financially stable. Boys will still be there when it's all done." But what parents don't realize is that their kids have to get out there and experience things on their own; all they can do is tell them instead of demanding them. Lani probably wished she would have listened, but things happen. Nobody really ever takes the advice they receive, hence the name advice; that's just how things work.

That night, after Lee calmed down, she had a long, hard talk with Lani. As usual, Lee did all the talking and Lani listened. She hated to see her mother cry and most of the time, she wouldn't even cry along with her. It wasn't that she didn't care; it was just something she did rarely when she talked with her mother. Lee basically told her she had her whole life ahead of her, she was young and she had six months of high school left. Her mom wasn't promoting abortion, as she was with her daughter on whatever she decided, but Lani didn't want a baby at that time and she didn't want a baby by Derek for that matter. She couldn't help but wonder if that was the reason it wasn't meant for them to have sex in the first place. She kept the original decision she decided the moment she knew she was pregnant – get an abortion.

She went to the doctor the next day with Lee and her father to see how far along she was. She couldn't get an ultrasound in the office; she had to go to the hospital. When the doctor (the same one who did the pregnancy test) felt Lani's belly, she made the assumption that she was due any day based on where it felt like her uterus was. Lani was upset and she knew that couldn't be right. That sparked a new problem. For one, her mom and dad were upset again because she was about due and her baby received no prenatal care. For two, everyone questioned whether Derek was the father. Lee was with her daughter the whole way; she wasn't really angry anymore.

Once her mother knew she was about to be a grandmother, she prepared for the newborn child. She prayed the child would be fine since it had no prenatal care, especially since Lani was smoking and doing whatever else she didn't know about. The whole family knew about the pregnancy after that. They were all stunned that Lani was pregnant because they didn't expect her to become pregnant at an early age. With all the discipline Lee gave, they damn sure thought she would be too scared to even have sex in the first place. They also made the mistake of placing her on a pedestal because she got good grades and was accepted to colleges, so in their eyes, she was an "angel" who could do no wrong. They all stopped by to visit Lani and made sure she was okay. They assured her that everything would be fine and now was the time to grow up. They warned her that she was no longer a child and everything had to be put on hold to tend to her child. They also questioned her about who her baby's father was since the time frame she gave them when she had sex with Derek, wasn't matching with her due date, but Lani kept her ground; no one was not going to tell her Derek wasn't the baby's father.

When Lani got the ultrasound two days later, she was amazed to see the life inside her body. The baby was no longer an embryo; it was a baby – a fully developed one. It looked as if it were sucking its thumb. But Lani felt at ease when she found out something she already knew – she was only five months pregnant. That brought some closure to her because she knew damn well she wasn't eight months, and she knew Derek was the father. After he found out she was eight months, he started saying the baby wasn't his. Although he was just being a man and not allowing a chick to get over on him by pinning a baby on him that wasn't his, that made her hate him forever because she knew what she was talking about. From that day on, she never spoke to him again, and never gave him an explanation as to why; even when he tried to make amends. She was not one of those females from the Maury Show who test like nine different guys and still don't find the father. She knew who her donor was. Lani's next step was to abort the pregnancy. The question though, was where. No place in Connecticut performed abortions with the female that far along. But after aggressively searching the internet for abortion centers in New York, Lani found what she was looking for. She had to get in soon though because in about one more week and two days, she would be too far along to go anywhere. She was able to get an appointment in three days.

Over those three days, her family tried to talk her out of it, but Lani had her mind made up. Shit, they didn't have to take care of it. She had it in her mind that she wasn't having that baby, especially the way Derek was acting; but even if he wanted it, she wasn't

62

keeping it. What they were saying to her had no impact on her and she felt no remorse at the time. Lee didn't want Lani to have the baby either but she also wasn't trying to persuade her to abort it. She also made sure her daughter wanted to go through with the abortion, telling her she may think about it later on in life and have regrets. She knew Lani was a smart girl who could be whatever she wanted in life and having a baby would slow her process down. So Lani and Lee took the road trip to New York and aborted the pregnancy. She did not want to get herself in that predicament ever again. She felt she not only let her mother down, but also herself.

Chapter Six: Whipped

Lani was feeling better than ever. She wasn't pregnant anymore, so she wasn't as tired and lazy now. She was back to her normal self. She felt pretty again; she had a rough month. She got caught smoking, her mother now knew she was having sex, she got pregnant, and she lost her father again because he disowned her. He began telling people she was nine months pregnant and was due to have a baby before he even knew she was really five months. That leaked out in the streets and everybody knew she was pregnant; she thought her life couldn't get any worse. Nothing really changed though. She was still smoking, still fucking, still doing her. About a month after the abortion, Donell came back into the picture. After being away for about two months, he began calling again.

Since Lani wasn't really talking to any guys at that time, she started talking to Donell a little more. This time, she found him more interesting than before. Of course she sexed him, probably a little quicker than usual but he was talking like his sex game was off the hook so she had to test it; and she was backed up so she wanted it anyway. The first time was not what she expected and he probably felt the same way. He was trying to beat the pussy down too much cause it getting dry. She thought that would be their last time, but it most certainly was not.

It was now two months before prom time. Lani was in search of a date. She wanted to ask Donell but at the time they weren't speaking, so she asked Cuda (her middle school crush) out the blue.

64

He agreed and from that moment, they began talking on the phone again. They were older now, so Cuda wasn't playing anymore games with Lani. He wanted to tap that ass since middle school and so did she, but she didn't want him as much as she did when they were younger. They talked on the phone every other day for about three weeks. One night, Lani snuck him in through her bedroom window and they got it on. He was moving entirely too fast though. He was trying to kill it. She thought her mother heard them because the bed was shaking loudly. He popped the condom trying to rip the pussy. He did not fuck Lani good and in return she couldn't fuck him good because there was more pain than pleasure so she couldn't get into it. After he came, he just left. No conversation (not that Lani wanted that, she wanted him to leave right after anyway), no thank you, no nothing. He really just gave her a hard dick and bubble gum (actually, she didn't even get the bubble gum).

They didn't talk again until the prom. He did keep his word and took her to the prom. Marie and Nisha didn't have dates, so Marie rode with Cuda and Lani, and Nisha rode with some homegirls of hers. On the way to the prom, Cuda rolled a blunt and got Lani and Marie high. They didn't want to be high at the prom, but they were. They looked so stupid when they entered. They thought everyone knew they were high and they knew they smelled like weed, so they just took a few pictures and sat down just observing the scenery – looking stupid. You would have thought Lani went without a date because he wasn't with her at all the whole night; he was with his boys. He didn't even take professional pictures with her. It became clear to her that he used her to show off with his boys; since he didn't go to the school, he wouldn't have been able to go to the prom without her or anyone else. He was doing his own thing; he even got a few numbers. She didn't leave with him either; so much for having a good night at the prom. She probably should have saved the wack session she had with him for prom night, at least then they both would have had something to look forward to, and maybe then he would have paid attention to her at the prom since he knew he would get some afterwards.

Marie was pregnant during prom time. It was her third pregnancy and she had no kids. Marie told Lani she purposely got pregnant because she didn't want to have her period around prom time because that's when it was due. Since she was wearing a white dress, she felt having her period would ruin her night. Though she did think about keeping it, she chose to abort it.

Donell was always in and out Lani's life. They would be on good terms for about a month and beef for about two. He was heavily in the streets trying to come up. They weren't speaking before the prom, but afterwards, he popped back up. Lani believed he did that so she wouldn't ask him to the prom. He wasn't anyone she was emotionally attached to, so him coming around here and there didn't bother her. She heard about his girlfriend and she even heard she was pregnant (which made her a little jealous), but his girlfriend didn't keep the baby. When she asked him about the pregnancy, he told her he didn't want her to keep it because they weren't together and he wasn't ready anyway. He lured Lani back into his life because he offered to pay for her $200 dress she got made for the prom and didn't pay the tailor for. She never got the money though, but she continued to deal with him. He was also on the bracelet at the time for a parole violation, so he was lonely and in need of companionship since he had a curfew.

Their sex life began to get better. Luckily she got on birth control after her pregnancy (which was her mother's idea) because he started fucking her raw. She was a bit naive in a way because this was the second time she thought the dude was using a condom – well he did but he claimed it popped and he didn't pull out. She kind of knew something wasn't right because the sex felt so good that she feel asleep. From that point on, what was the point of using a condom with him.

It was a couple days before graduation. Lani was proud of her accomplishments. She had finished high school at the top of her class. She graduated 12 out of 213 in her class and with a 3.2 GPA despite a few F's and D's she received during her last year (mainly due to skipping class). Lani, Nisha, and Marie were all at Nisha's house just chillin' having a girl's day. It was a beautiful spring day and they were getting high and telling jokes. One of Marie's homeboys called her on her cellphone and asked her could he come by. Kane was his name and he was fine.

Kane was about five years or four and a half years older than Lani. He was good friends with Torey, Marie's boyfriend, and he was also one of Tracey's (Torey's sister) baby's father. Lani had seen Kane before and she always thought he was blazin. He was caramel complexion, nice lips, good hair, and tall with a slim build. He wasn't a street dude, though he tried to get his hustle on, but when it came to beef and poppin' them thangs, he was the pussy type; he definitely wouldn't be able to protect a girlfriend of his.

Kane had a lot of drama in his life with his baby's mother being a psycho and he wasn't even swinging the dick her way anymore from what she [Lani] was told. Even before this, Lani knew about the fights and crazy shit his baby's mother would do from Marie. Not to mention he still lived under his mother's roof (who Lani heard was a dike from Marie who got her information from Tracey) and wouldn't even allow him to have female company. Kane talked on the phone with Nisha before, it was nothing major but she did have a little crush on him. They never got up with each other, never kissed, and never fucked. Nisha was the hard-to-get kind anyway (not that Lani or Marie was easy) and she was picky with her men, so nothing got to jump off between the two. At this point in time, she may have had one piece of dick, which was excellent; not too many females were able to hold out until junior year in high school.

When Kane arrived to Nisha's house, Nisha chose not to go outside so just Lani and Marie went out. After talking with him for about ten minutes, Marie realized his only purpose for coming there was to get at Lani. Lani wasn't paying him any attention though; except for the occasional peeks at him in admiration of his beauty. Lani had on short shorts and a tank top. She may have been petite, but she had a decent body. She had enough meat on her bones and she had a nice fat ass to go along with that. She may not have had the biggest chest but her personality and beauty made up for it; dudes always told her there was something about her. Although she thought Kane was cute, she never thought she would be able to pull him. For one, she didn't think she was his type and for two, she was seventeen and he was twenty-two. But Marie did tell Lani he was feeling her. Lani just smiled and she was surprised. He offered her a ride home and she took it. He took her number and the rest was history.

It was now graduation day. Lani finally did it; she completed the biggest challenge of her life. She had the longest four years of her life. Her years in high school played a major part in her life and she learned a lot. She also made Lee proud since the only thing she ever wanted her daughter to do was to graduate. Right before she left her home to walk across the stage, she received a call from

Kane. He wasn't aware she was about to graduate and he was trying to get up with her; but she told him she was graduating and he told her he'd catch her at a later date.

That later date would be two days after she graduated. He called her, they talked for a few, and then he picked her up. Talking with Kane was good for Lani because it would be her way of getting over Donell and washing him out her life. Donell was a grimy nigga. At the time, he was fucking madd bitches and leading Lani on. He was also still fucking with his childhood sweetheart. He wouldn't admit it but she always would be wifey; after all, he was messing with her since they were fifteen. Lani didn't like being second either, but there was something about him that kept her to him, even if she knew she was second.

As Lani and Kane drove through the city, they talked and tried to get to know each other, but there was more silence than talking. He rolled up two "L's" (weed) with her. He had her high as hell because normally she would only smoke half the blunt, but she didn't want to seem like a chump if she told him she didn't want to smoke anymore. She was high as hell. She still hadn't learned her lesson of being an amateur and smoking with a professional. She wasn't really an amateur, but she wasn't as advanced as Kane – in any department for that matter. That was probably his motive from the beginning to get her high because then he asked if she was ready to go home. *This nigga is crazy. He want me to go home high like this to my mother, yeah right. If only he knew her, he would not have asked me that,* Lani thought. So she told him No. They rode around for about another fifteen minutes and then he took her to his house. They were both high; she was obviously higher than him. They relaxed in his house, watching TV alone; his mother (who Lani heard

69

was strict) was out and about. They fell asleep only to be awakened by his mother coming home about two in the morning.

They stayed asleep, well at least she did and that's when he took advantage of her. He started touching her and then put his hands down her pants. She pretended to be sleep but she knew what was going on. He eventually got her pants off, put a condom on and started fucking her. She damn sure wanted it, but not like that, it was too late. It wasn't all that good either. Lani had yet to get a nigga who put it down the first time.

She stayed the night and left about seven in the morning. Lani didn't want her mother to know about the guys she dealt with. She was never with someone with a car, so everytime Kane dropped her off, she would have him drop her off around the corner at apartment buildings that she told him was her aunt's house. She would walk in the building as if it really was her aunt's house and when he left she would walk to her house so her mother wouldn't hear a car in the front of the house and look out the window. When she got in the house, she heard it from her mother.

"Where have you been?" Lee asked in an abrupt tone of voice.

"I stayed at Nisha house, I fell asleep over there." Lani replied. Lee knew she was lying, and she made it known.

"Yeah whatever Lani, I hope that nigga you laying up with let you stay with him when I kick your ass out." Lani was shocked at the statement but amused at the same time. She just walked to her room. Lee at this point was fed up with her daughter, but she didn't give up on her. Although she wanted Lani to live her life the way she wanted, she knew that was a fantasy and if she waited patiently, Lani would turn out to be what she wanted, or at least close.

Lani continued her relationship with Kane. The second meeting at his house was a little different. His mother was out of town for a few days so they had the house to themselves. They relaxed on the sofa watching a few movies, smoking and drinking – basically getting nice. Once he felt nice enough, he invited her upstairs to his bedroom. He didn't turn any lights on; he just got straight to the point. He took her pants off and began sucking on her titties and fondling her. Then he did something she was not thinking of, he ate her pussy, and he ate it good. He sucked the juices out her pussy like he was eating an orange. It was so good, and he got her pussy so wet that he wasn't about to let that pussy go dry by putting a condom on. Lani was usually good about telling men to put a condom on, but Kane ate her pussy so good, she wasn't about to mess the mood up. He tore the pussy up too – in a gentle way. This time was 150% better than the first time and it was worth trying a second time; he also was worth getting in trouble for. He made her cum about four times. Throughout the night he also fucked her over and over again. He would wake up out his sleep and slip back into her; both on their sides, and that turned her on even more. This was the best sex she ever experienced. She was officially hooked on him.

Lani didn't tell Marie and Nisha she was fucking Kane – at least not right away. She held it inside, sex that good had to be kept a secret. She didn't have any particular reason as to why she didn't tell them, that's just what she chose to do. Besides, friends don't tell their friends everything, regardless of what you think. Lani began to gain feelings for Kane; she actually thought she loved him in such a short amount of time. She was bugging, but she had never been with an older nigga and she damn sure never had a nigga put it down so hard that she thought about it the next day. Lust is almost as dangerous as love.

Lani hadn't talked to Nisha in weeks. It made it seem as if Lani was guilty being that Nisha talked to Kane on the phone a couple of times, but Lani felt as if she didn't do anything wrong. She stayed in touch with Marie though, and Marie would constantly ask why she didn't call Nisha. Lani would simply reply, "she didn't call me." Lani and Nisha did eventually talk again and all Nisha did was make jokes about the situation, but the jokes had some truth in it. Lani apologized to Nisha and told her she didn't think anything of it because they never did anything. They patched up their differences and things were back to normal. It was nothing close to what Reasha did so it was easy for Nisha to forgive and forget.

Lani and Kane began to chill more often. Everyday when he got off work at 3:30, they would hang out and play basketball together. She thought their relationship reminded her of the movie "Love and Basketball"; but it was no where near that. He came over often at night when Lee was asleep. Since he was older, she felt it appropriate that he sneak in through the back door rather than the window; she left the window for the young boys.

One night, he didn't really want to come over. They were on the phone and Lani was trying to get him to come over so he could put it on her again. He kept telling her no, until finally he replied, "alright, but you have to do whatever I tell you to." Lani knew exactly what that meant so she told him "yeah" just to get him over there. When he finally arrived, she was excited. They rested for a few and got down to the get down. He kissed her all over, ate her pussy then wanted her to return the favor. She was disgusted, even though she already knew what he wanted before he got there. She was so hooked on him and the sex was so good, she almost did it. She was never into that, but he had to have something so good that made her even consider it, but she replied to him nicely, "I'm not into that. I don't do that." So they resumed their normal activity and that was that.

As time went on, Lani found herself gaining more and more feelings for Kane. The streets knew they were fucking too. She actually thought Kane had feelings for her, but that was just a thought. Truth of the matter, he just wanted to fuck her and he got what he wanted; sooner than later, he would show his ass.

Tracey heard about the relationship with Lani and Kane. She never knew the validity of what she heard until one day when Tracey's mother rolled up on them in the car together. Her mother wanted to talk to Kane about his son and some pamper shit. Lani knew Tracey's mother and she didn't care if she saw them together because from what she knew, Kane and Tracey were not together. Tracey and Lani were never cool and they didn't even speak. They only knew each other on the strength of Marie.

When Tracey's mother confirmed the rumors to her daughter, Tracey grew hatred for Lani and forever would hate her for fucking her baby's father. Lani never understood why she was so mad being that they never even knew each other, only by faces and names, and she and Kane were a done deal. But actions like those were typical of young girls, anybody who fucked their baby's father they did not like, whether known or unknown. From an analytical point of view, one could say it is difficult to embrace someone who slept with their baby's father.

By this time, Nisha and Marie knew about Lani and Kane. Lani told Marie more details than Nisha, but of course Marie told Nisha. Lani was hooked on him; he had her nose wide open. It was her birthday, she was now 18, and able to go into the store and buy

Dutches for her weed. She hung out with Kane on her birthday. He told her he would get her a gift in a couple of days but that gift never came. Kane's birthday was exactly two weeks after Lani's and she brought him a pair of white and gray high top air force one's. Marie was upset with Lani because Lani was never the type to be spending money on guys. Besides, he didn't even get her a gift for her birthday. He didn't hustle anymore after he did three years in jail six years prior, but he did have a good paying job. Marie saw the dog in Kane and she was upset at how he had her friend wrapped around his finger, but that was the same way Lani felt about Torey. It's funny how the tables turn.

The night of his birthday, Lani wanted Kane to come over. She paged him off the hook and received no return call. Finally a call came through from an unknown number. She was sure it was Kane. She picked up the phone only to realize the voice on the other end was that of a female. "Somebody called Kane?" The girl asked.

"Yeah, is he around?" Lani replied with confidence.

"He busy, you gon' have to call him tomorrow." Lani was crushed. She never had that happen before. She wanted to cry, but she just went to sleep.

The next day Kane called her to cop a plea. He told her some bullshit about how his ex-girlfriend was at his house the prior night talking with his mother (he wasn't there) and she took his beeper and was calling numbers back. That was so lame. He had over twelve hours to come up with an excuse and that was what he came up with? Lani knew it was bullshit, but she still continued to mess with him. She recalled all the times when Marie was being stupid for Torey and how she would tell her she stupid and Nisha would tell her to leave him alone. Now, they were saying that to her. Nisha was probably happy Lani was going through it and not her. After that

74

incident, she began to really see who he really was and realized she had been gamed all along. She wanted the sneakers she brought him back after that because all she could think about was how he was fucking someone else in the sneakers she brought him.

One day when she skipped out on work and Kane thought she was at work, she walked back over to the hood, only to see Kane ride by with a girl in the car. Again, Lani was heartbroken. When she asked him about it, he gave a bullshit ass excuse once again. She was supposedly a girl he was giving a ride for his mother.

Lani began to not like Leos. She wasn't good with Leos. Donell was a Leo and Kane was a Leo. Leos were liars in her world and they had game for days. Shit, she was a Leo and she had some game with her. Lani didn't want to deal with Kane anymore and she didn't. He was a whore. She was also upset that Tracey began to not like her, even though she and Lani weren't friends and she wasn't with Kane. She wasn't upset because Tracey was someone important in her life because she could care less about the broad; Lani just didn't like drama and she always avoided it in every possible way.

She didn't like how she was used and abused by Kane either. She thought he liked her. The last draw came when she found out from Marie that he was still with his girlfriend whom he'd been with for three years. Tracey and she even had a few fallouts behind him and didn't like each other because of that. *When did he have time for her*, Lani thought, recalling all their moments together. He would chill with Lani and spend the night with her also, so where did the other chick get time from him? Although Lani was hurt, it was all a learning experience for her. It was her first official time being a fool for someone. She thought she was in love but it was only lust. She was just in love with his magic wand.

75

Immediately following Kane, Donell popped back into her life. Donell knew about Kane and often saw them together. Lani showed no shame in having Kane pick her up and drop her off at Marie's aunt's restaurant which was on Donell's part of town; he even popped in the restaurant from time to time to see Marie or Lani if she was there. He seemed jealous when he would see Lani with Kane but being a man, he didn't admit it. Since they were cool with each other and had a platonic relationship, she began telling him how she was used and abused. He gave her a hug and asked her if he could come over later. She told him "yeah" and thought, *what a sweetheart.* He may not have been shit, but at least he tried to be a gentleman and didn't really sweat the fact that she went off with another dude.

Lani was fed up with guys up to this point, but she still resumed relations with Donell. She continued to hang out in the neighborhood also. She was having problems with her mother and her mother was getting more and more fed up. Hurt and confused, she decided to go a different route. She decided since she hung in the streets everyday and in the hood, she might as well make a little money too; make it worth being in the streets. She always kept a job, which her mother instilled in her early on to have her own money. She had a different mission though; she wanted fast money, fuck a paycheck.

Chapter Seven: Hustlin' is in the blood

Lani was upset at the way she had been used and abused by men, but that was life. She felt insecure at this point. She didn't feel pretty anymore, so one day she decided to make a big change in her life.

Lani and Marie had been attending college not too far from their high school. Although Lani was accepted to out of state colleges such as St. John's, Morris Brown, Duquesne, and Howard, she decided to stay home for a year to make some money to take with her so there would be less of a struggle. They had only been attending Southern Connecticut State University for about ten days when Lani woke up one morning to a disturbing reality. When she first heard, "two planes have knocked down the World Trade Centers" on the news and observed fire coming from the two tallest buildings in New York, she didn't really think anything of it. She got dressed and was ready to continue her college life without the thought of terrorists.

When she left the house and began to walk to school, it hit her. *We're at WAR*, she thought. Lani never thought she would be living during war. She thought this was the end of the world. She just knew one day she would walk out the door and there would be men with guns shooting and killing people. She especially thought her life would be over because she was an African-American. At that point, she thought, *fuck school, the world is about to end*.

Lani withdrew from school without telling Lee. She told the school director she had family who died in 9-11 so she wouldn't get a penalty for dropping out late. It wasn't the right thing to say, but everyone capitalizes off a disaster, especially the government. She began to sit back and analyze her life. She decided that life goes on regardless of what. As long as her heart was beating and her brain was functioning, she was going to continue living. She declared from that day on, it was *fuck niggas, get money.* So she decided she wanted to hustle.

She began selling crack cocaine in her hood. She had a job working at Starbucks Coffee, but that was chump change to her. She had an "expensive" lifestyle to support and a reputation to maintain, and $7.75 an hour just wasn't supporting it. Of course when she started, she didn't make it known. She didn't want neither Marie nor Nisha to find out and she damn sure didn't want Lee to find out. She still didn't have that much freedom back at home anyway, so she had to do her thing discreetly. That all changed however, when Lee and Lani had a big argument and Lee slapped Lani.

Lani was upset because here she was, eighteen years old and her mother was still putting her hands on her. So when Lee left, so did she, but she planned on leaving for good. She packed all her clothes in trashbags and left Lee a note. In the note, she explained how she was fed up with the lack of freedom she received, the abuse, and everything else she disagreed with. She decided to stay at Nisha's house (which was right around the corner), but then she decided that wasn't such a good idea because she knew that would be the first place she would check. So she just kept her clothes there and went there late at night when she knew Lee would not be out the house.

When Lee got home and read the letter, she was angry, crying and searching for her daughter. She called Nisha, Marie, family, anyone she could think of and everyone said they didn't know

78

where Lani was. Lani managed to elude her mother for about four days. She would go to the "G" where she knew most of the guys. She would go out there and play dice and also managed to inconspicuously sell her product. After a few days, word got out to Marie from a guy friend of hers who lived in the "G", that Lani was selling drugs. Marie laughed at her friend because she was always getting into something. She was always the one who thought outside the box and was willing to try anything (well not anything) to get money. When Lani was approached by Marie and she asked her if she was hustling, she just laughed and told her "no".

Marie's family didn't like Lani too much. They thought she influenced Marie to do the things she was doing like smoking, having sex, and God knows what else in the street. Little did they know, Marie's first time smoking was not with Lani, she had sex before Lani and anything else she did, she did it because she wanted to. If anything, she had Lani doing shit too. Even Marie's father thought Lani was a bad influence. They looked at Lani as the child who had no home training and would never be anything in life. She was a tomboy and didn't have a care in the world about life. They would often talk about her and did not want Marie to hang around Lani, but as stated previously, Marie did what Marie wanted to do.

Lani figured Lee had stopped searching for her by the fourth day, so she was hanging out at Nisha's, when Lee popped up. Nisha's mom was preparing to give Lani a perm. She was basing her edges with Vaseline as Lee was pulling up. Nisha, Nisha's mom, and Marie persuaded Lani to go out and talk to her and tell her she wasn't ready to go home. *Easy for them bitches to say, they don't know my mother*, Lani thought. She talked to her mom and told her she was about to get a perm. That upset Lee and she told her daughter to get her ass in the car right now. Lani had no choice but to listen, after all, that was her mother. She gathered her belongings and left. Boy, did she hear it like she never heard it before when they got home.

Lee was very disappointed and she felt disrespected. Lani just sat there listening. Lee was crying, pouring her heart out to her while she just sat and showed no emotion. When Lee finally calmed down, she apologized and began talking to her more calmly. They both came to an agreement, but when all was said and done; Lee still put her on punishment. No phone, no TV, and definitely no outside. Lee also expressed anger towards Lani's friends for lying to her about her whereabouts. Lani was unsure as to why Lee would think her friends would rat her out.

Although her actions were negative, they turned out to produce positive results. Lee gave Lani more freedom and didn't put her hands on her anymore. With that said and done, Lani still hit the block, this time back in her old hood, the "Tre."

What made her confident about hustling was because there was another female younger than her hustling. Manny, the one who she smoked with when she first got high, hustled for years before Lani. She also had a few cases too. That didn't stop Lani though. She felt she could hustle smarter than Manny, and that she did.

When Lani first hit the strip, she vowed to only hustle during sundown. That way, with less light, she was less identifiable. *No face, no case,* was her motto. That soon changed quickly when she quit her job and decided to hustle full-time. That's where being a tomboy really mattered. She wore baggy jeans, sneakers, a big hoody and a baseball cap. She kept her hair wrapped in a scarf and the hat on her head, along with the hoody. The only people who knew who she was were the ones who knew her. She had the fiends refer to her as "SONNY." Basically, she fooled authorities by posing as a male.

While hustling, Lani began to make a little money; and you know what more money bring – more problems. Niggas in the hood began to become jealous. They felt their pockets become lighter. All or the majority of the fiends would go to Lani for their "medicine". She had a pretty good connect, so she was one of the few with the potent product in the hood. As the niggas began getting jealous, the threats started to come.

They would tell Marie to tell Lani they were going to rob her or shoot her if she didn't stop hustling. Marie would relay the message and she and Lani would just laugh at how niggas could hate on a female. Lani would reply in a cocky manner, "they just mad I'm a chick and I'm seeing it more than them. I only been here a couple of weeks and seen more paper than they ever would."

Somehow word got back to Donell about Lani hustling. To think he would try to encourage her not to do that, he damn near praised her as if she should have been in the game a long time ago. Donell wasn't cool with niggas from the "Tre," because he was from the "Hill;" so getting money in that area was out of the question. She hadn't talked to him in some weeks and now when he does pop up, he wants her to sell for him. She was upset with his proposal, but she thought, *what the hell, nothing wrong with a couple extra dollars*, so she accepted. He didn't give her crack though; he gave her fourteen bags of weed. He told her to give him one hundred dollars back and she could keep forty. She smoked some and sold some. She dodged Donell for a couple more weeks. She fucked up his product but he got what he deserved for trying to pimp her; she wasn't anybody's damn mule. When she finally got up with him, she gave him the hundred dollars but he was mad she took so long to sell

81

fourteen bags. They would end up beefing again for a couple of weeks.

She continued to hustle. By now, old timers began to recognize what she was doing. These were old timers who knew Lee. Eventually word got back to Lee but she never asked Lani about it, so Lani never knew she knew. She only had the thought her mother knew because her youngest uncle called her from jail and told her he heard she was out there hustlin'. She denied allegations and that was that.

Things really began to heat up in the hood. The niggas started beefing with another territory across town, which wasn't unusual. "Tre" niggas, or the "Tre bloods" as they called themselves, were the grimest niggas in New Haven at this time. They were notorious for robbing, mainly because most of them were broke. But what they didn't know or didn't take heed to was that beefing only made you broker.

New Haven was a small town thirty minutes from Connecticut's capital city, Hartford. Over recent years, their murder rate rised, mainly because of the little niggas coming off the porch trying to make a name for themselves. Everybody knew everybody and if you weren't known, you were known by face or someone in your surroundings was known. Aside from that, everybody was fucking everybody; it was nothing but a cycle. Once one chick was done with somebody, she was fucking with somebody else. It got to the point where you was like, *Damn, wasn't he just fucking with such and such last week, and ain't she pregnant by such and such and she fucking with this dude.* Or, *Damn, who he or she gon' be fucking with next? It ain't too many more left to choose from.*

There weren't many places you could go to and have a good time because someone would always ruin it and the event would be shut down. If it wasn't niggas fighting or shooting over whatever, it was bitches fighting over what nigga belonged to who. Their annual parade, The Freddy Fixer held in May, was a fashion show which included violence because of all the territories joining together in one place. You couldn't be off point at the Freddy or you might become an innocent victim. As long as you stayed on point and aware of what was going on around you, you were good; if you saw people running, you didn't care what they were running for, you knew it wasn't good and you would ask questions later. Most of the clubs had been shut down because of violence. Most of the beefs, when completely thought about its origination, were either over money, or the opposite sex. There were a few that resulted over nothing –"the just because" beefs.

New Haven was broken up into different territories. The hoods were the "Tre," the "G," the "Island," the "Jungle," the "Hill," the "Ville," the "Tribe," and "West Hills." When someone asked you where you were from, those were the areas you would say. Of those hoods, the "Tre" was only cool with niggas from the "G." Their strongest beef was with "Ville" niggas. The "Tre" was the most hated gang in all of New Haven. Niggas from other sides viewed them as being grimy and not loyal. If "Tre" niggas were in sight, you better believe there was a gun in sight too and somebody was schemin' on somebody.

Despite everything going on in the hood, Lani continued her quest without threat. She felt the world was coming to an end and she felt lonely in the world, so she didn't care if she went to jail or whatever else. She was truly a "Black Girl Lost."

One day, Marie and Lani were on the phone talking. Marie began telling Lani about a new drug her cousin, D-Man, was telling her about. They were both laughing saying he was crazy. Marie connected him in the conversation and he started telling them about the drug.

D-Man was one of the live niggas in the hood. He hung with Lani's cousin J-Real. Together them dudes were dangerous with the guns and the women. D-Man had recently been released from jail after a shooting when he was sixteen. J-Real was out on bond for an attempted murder. D-Man was handsome though. He was a nice brown complexion, nice and tall – the kind of tall that a female puts her arms around his neck, stands on her tippy toes and he lowers a little so they could kiss one another – Sexy. He would always flirt with Lani and tell her he'd break her back, put it on her, and he would make his dick game sound so good. So good even Marie would want a piece from her own cousin. At the time, Lani and Marie compared him to Ja Rule because he would always talk about his dick game. But D-Man was off limits. He was Roni's boyfriend.

D-Man told them about ecstasy. Marie and Lani heard of "X" before but they thought only white people took it, they were unaware it was an addiction in the hood. But indeed it was, if a gangsta nigga like D-Man taking "X," it must have been something. He went on about it telling them weed had nothing on "X" and how they would be able to smoke twenty blunts and it would be nothing, but his persuasions were to no avail. They thought it would be the same as smoking crack but in pill form, so he wasn't able to pressure them.

Lani was content with the money she was making. Though it was nothing to brag about, it was quick and it was more than her checks from Starbucks. She decided to take a trip to the City to get some gear she so desperately needed. She took the trip with D-Man and Marie. They took the train and they shopped. During their trip, Marie decided to get a tattoo. It would be her first and she wanted to do it. Lani had been there done that. When she was sixteen, her mother treated her to a tattoo for her birthday.

D-Man and Marie went to Harlem Tattoos to get the tattoo while Lani did some more shopping. When she arrived at the tattoo place, she couldn't believe the tattoo Marie wanted to get. Being the careless person she was, as she would even misplace money, she forgot her ID. She asked Lani to borrow hers so she could get the tattoo and at first Lani refused. She did not want Marie to get Torey's name on her body because he was not worth it. After a while, Lani just said, "fuck it, it ain't me," and let Marie borrow her ID. D-Man coached her the whole way and ensured her *Pain is Love*, which only encouraged her decision even more. When it was all said and done and the pain was over, Marie had the playboy bunny symbol with Torey's name engraved inches away from her pussy. Lani couldn't believe it; her girl was really in love.

Things began to really get real in the hood. After all the niggas went out to a bar one night, they came back to the hood the next day saying there was a big fight with "West Hills" niggas. During the scuffle, a "Tre" nigga was shot in the leg. He survived but they were planning retaliation. Lani and Marie didn't think anything of it and they continued to hang out in the hood. Nobody really seemed to care that one of their own just got shot, everyone just resumed regular activity.

It was unusually live the day after the shooting. It was Friday and money was being made, everybody was humble and chilling in the park. D-Man introduced Marie to his new shorty Candy. D-Man and Roni (Lani and Marie's friend) had broken up after he caught her with another nigga at her house, so he moved on; even though he was messing with Candy while he was with Roni, but now he made it known.

85

Although it was a chilly October day, it felt like summer because it was so live. When it became dark, Lani and Marie left the hood to hang out with one of their homeboys D-Right. D-Right drove them around a little, smoked with them and vibed as they drove across town to talk with some other dudes they all knew. As the night went on, it became colder. Lani didn't have her coat because she left it in the hood at Nisha's cousin house. Since it was cold, Lani was ready to leave and Marie wanted to catch her visit (Torey was in jail for shooting someone over a dice game,so she would visit him often).

D-Right dropped them back off in the hood across the street from the "hood store." The store was unusually populated and everything seemed normal. Lani told D-Right thanks, told Marie to call her and she walked about a mile to get her coat and bike. On her way out to go back to the store, she saw a fiend. She served the fiend in the alley and continued her journey. When she returned seconds later, she was shocked at what she saw. There were crowds of people outside as she approached the block the store was on and saw red and blue lights flashing. What she found out next should have changed her life.

There was a shooting just that quick at the store where she was dropped off at and about to return to. Apparently, "West Hills," or "Wild Wild West" as they called it, had unfinished business. They came back with submachine guns and automatic weapons and tore the streets up. They shot seven people, but of the seven people, none of them were the ones involved in the scuffle the night before. One of them was a female who everyone thought was Lani since she hung in that area so frequently. It was unfortunate, but luckily only one person died; a man who didn't have anything to do with it, just

86

going to the store. In fact, none of the men who were involved in the fight the previous night were even around that area.

That shook Lani's bones. She was spared possible death by a coat, bike, and crack cocaine. Had she had her coat and bike and never left with D-Right, she and Marie may have been dead. She took it as a blessing and felt it wasn't her time to go. She still hustled though. The next week would turn out to be a very dramatic week. That very next day, Lani hung out with D-Man, Manny, and another dude. Life was beginning to get rough and Lani didn't know where her life was going.

D-Man, Manny, and the other dude decided they wanted to pop an "X." They pressured Lani into getting one. Since she was going through so much, she thought, *what the hell.* They brought the e pill, popped it, and were dropped off back to the hood. Lani went to a basehead's house in the hood to bag up her re-up. As she was nearly finished, she began to feel weird. She had forgotten about the e pill. Her eyes became fully dilated, and her head became light. She started feeling powerful inside that small bathroom where she was bagging up. All of a sudden, she began talking to herself. "Yeah, I'm about to get this motherfuckin' money, get this money, ain't nobody gon' stop me." She repeated that numerous times until she was finally done baggin' up. When she was done, she stood up, looked in the mirror at herself, and stared silently until she was interrupted two minutes later by a knock on the door. It was Manny.

"You ready." Manny asked.

"Yeah, I'm ready." Lani replied.

"Damn, look at your eyes. You feeling that shit."

"Yeah, I'm feeling it." They both laughed. "I feel good as hell." Lani hit the basehead off with two free bags and continued out the back door. Manny stayed as she had business to handle too.

Lani walked down the street fiercely. She felt like superwoman. She was walking and couldn't tell if she was walking hard or what, but she could hear her footsteps in her Tims. She continued and went to get her bike from her cousin's house. When she entered the house, she just walked over to her bike silently. Her whole expression changed as she just wanted to get her bike and keep it moving. She kept her head down most of the time in the house but one of her cousins couldn't help but ask,

"Lani, you okay?"

"Yeah, I'm alright." And she proceeded out the door. On her way down the street, she ran into her friend, Roni (D-Man's ex girlfriend). When she saw her, she ran over to her and gave her a big hug and kept telling her how much she loved her and they shared a laugh. Roni knew she had taken an e pill so she was just observing Lani and laughing. They all hopped in the car and went to Roni's house. On their way there, Roni lit up a blunt. It was Roni, Lani, Roni's sister Benz and Cuda's brother Len in the car. Roni passed the blunt to Lani who just kept smoking the blunt. Roni had to tell her to pass it or she would have smoked the blunt by her lonesome. Lani could never smoke a blunt like that. She usually took about four puffs and she was high. D-Man was right, weed had nothing on ecstasy. Her short experience with "X" made her forget about anything that was going on in her life.

The next day, Lani was telling Marie about her experience with ecstasy. "Yo, ecstasy is the shit Marie. You have to try it. I know we both were like yeah right, but it's the best high I ever had."

"Well what were you doing?" Marie asked curiously.

"Man, I felt like superman out that bitch last night. Yo, you say or do whatever you thinking. If you don't like somebody, you gonna tell them, fuck how they feel and if you love somebody, you gonna

88

tell them over and over again. And the weed...man I smoked with Roni and Benz last night, we smoked like ten blunts. I couldn't stop." Lani and Marie were laughing hysterically. "I'm not taking it anymore though, I'm straight."

That was a lie though, Lani did do "X" again, as a matter of fact, she did it about three more times. She finally stopped after the fourth time when she thought she was going to die. The world was spinning, she was hot, it felt like her brain was frying and she just looked stupid altogether. She was standing at the corner store, eyes wide open, when Nisha's aunt drove by. There was a traffic light at that corner so they were stuck at the light and usually Lani would embrace them, but when they spoke, she just nodded and turned away from them like they were enemies and she didn't even care. They just looked at her like she was on crack. After that, she quit. She didn't want to be in the hood looking like a crack head. She was selling it, but she didn't want to eventually begin using it.

The hood became "hot" after the shooting. There were police, detectives, and the Narcs all over trying to get to the bottom of the shooting that killed one and injured six innocent bystanders. When Lani went outside that Monday, she saw D-Man, Marie, and three other dudes in the car circling the block. They stopped on the corner to talk to Lani, and Marie and D-Man tried to get Lani to get in the car. She declined the offer but asked Marie to get out and walk with her. Marie agreed and the car proceeded to pull over. As they began to move, three cop cars rolled up on them. Lani didn't know what was happening. She was so scared that she threw her pack of crack down the sewer. She thought they were coming for her and did not want to be caught with any product on her. The cops swarmed on the car that Marie and D-Man were in and hopped out with their guns drawn, ordering them out the vehicle. Lani looked on wondering what the hell was going on. The cops cuffed all five occupants of the car as crowds gathered to look on. Someone called the cops and said someone in the car was flashing a gun out the window and circling the block. One of the men in the car did have a gun, but it was a fake gun. It was a fake submachine gun like the real one used in the shooting that past Friday. What a dummy. The cops took that seriously and arrested them all. As Marie sat on the curb handcuffed, Lani yelled and told her she was going to call her mother.

She ran to the payphone and called Marie's mom. Marie's mom hurried to the scene demanding an explanation. She was furious as she talked with Marie and then one of the cops. All of a sudden Marie's mom, Trina, came out of nowhere and began cursing Lani out. "This is all your fault. That is supposed to be you in that car, not my daughter. Ever since she started hanging with you, she been in nothing but trouble. You stay away from my daughter you hear me." Lani was so hurt she burst out crying. How was it her fault? She tried to get Marie out the car and besides, Marie was with her cousin D-Man, not her.

After that incident, Marie and Lani didn't talk for a few days. Things began to get crazy in the hood and the cops sent more undercovers than ever before. People were getting arrested everyday for making an undercover sale. One day when Lani was in a different part of the "Tre," she began arguing with another boy over a hundred dollar sale. They argued in front of the fiend until finally Lani gave up and let the boy get the sale. She would later learn the fiend was an undercover, because the boy was arrested a few days later. Lani found out the cops questioned the boy about who she was. Luckily for her, they asked him who the boy with the hoody was. The boy knew who they were asking about, but he chose not to

90

snitch. She knew then that they were on her and she had to chill.
She started hanging with Manny again after that.

Neither Lani nor Manny wanted to hang in the street, it was
too hot. So Manny started hanging with a homeboy of hers and Lani
traveled along too. She became cool with T-Rizz in just one
encounter. After that, it was Lani calling him to pick her up, not
Manny. She stopped hustling so she wasn't making any money.
She had quit her job so she definitely didn't have any income. She
started hanging with T-Rizz, his brother Llama, and some off T-Rizz's
friends in his van, which was like a living room on wheels. Lani used
T-Rizz to get out the streets. She didn't want to stay in the house
and she didn't want to be in the streets; so it worked out perfectly for
her hanging with him. She began hanging so tight with him that
people began thinking they were sleeping together.

There were times when Lani would be in the car with them
and she would see Donell. He began thinking something was up.
Donell knew T-Rizz and when he was at the car one day and saw T-
Rizz in the back with Lani and Llama driving with Tammy in the front,
he definitely knew something was up. That just didn't look right to
him and he wasn't trying to hear he was her friend. He later found
out Lani was holding his guns. Lani was also holding some guns for
Donell and as soon as he heard that, he got his guns from her and
didn't talk to her for a few days. He didn't want his guns getting
mixed up with anyone else's and he didn't want to deal with Lani
either.

After a while, she began to get uncomfortable. She was riding
around with a bunch of dudes who had guns and drugs in the car (as
if she wasn't accustomed to that already). T-Rizz had beef with a lot
of men and his van was not unknown. All she could think was *what if
somebody just shoot the car up with me in it or what if the cops pull*

91

the car over. It was crazy. One night, she almost became an innocent victim by one of her family members. They were riding up the street when a car started flagging them down. They didn't stop, they continued. The car kept flashing their lights at them. All of a sudden, T-Rizz and his boys started grabbing their guns from under the seat and they pulled over. Her heart was pounding. The car pulled up on the side of them. She saw the car out the window and thought it looked familiar, but when she heard her cousin start talking, she realized it was him. Her cousin pulled the car over to try to squash any beef between T-Rizz and his crew. Her cousin didn't see her because she was sitting in the back and the van had limo tints. Her cousin probably didn't even know they had guns ready for him and his other occupant of the car. God must have been with her, because nothing happened. She took her sign from the Lord and ran with it. From that point on, she slowly created distance between she and T-Rizz.

Lani didn't want to live her life that way anymore and she began looking for another job. When Marie told Nisha about everything that was going on, Nisha told Lani she was going to call her mother and tell her. Although Lani took that as a sign that she cared for her, she did not want her telling her mother anything she was doing because it was her business; she didn't want anyone calling her mother to tell her anything because it wasn't anyone's place to – if she wasn't dead or they weren't calling to say hi, there was no need to call.

Around this time, Marie had been getting lonely from the absence of her boyfriend. He had been down for a minute, often telling her he would be out soon. He concealed the fact that he had been sentenced to four years and in an effort to get her to wait for him, he kept her thinking he would be getting out soon. He needed to be in jail anyway, or else he would have been dead. He had been on a robbing spree along with another male friend of the crew named Deshawn. Deshawn was also from the "Tre" and he attended the same middle school with the girls. Feeding her needs, Marie decided to get involved with somebody else. Though it started as a sex thing, she quickly became hooked on Reno. Reno worked with her and he had a girlfriend at the time. He was handsome, resembling Allen Iverson, but he was a herb ass nigga. Normally Marie may not have looked his way, but her hormones were raging and his constant testosterone presence made her start looking.

If only guys knew the things females do, they would probably be more on point. The first time Marie and Reno had sex, Lani was in the next room. Lani happened to be at Marie's house and told her she would stay the night since her parents were on vacation. After smoking, Lani got lazy and fell asleep in Marie's bed. After Marie talked to Reno and invited him over, Marie woke Lani up and made her sleep on her mother's bed. Reno wanted to keep his infidelity on the low and had he known Lani was there, he may not have come. Though Lani was tired, she did here Reno scream like a bitch when he came.

It only took Lani a few weeks to not like Reno. He reminded her of Kane with his sneaky ways. He was older than Marie and Lani sensed he was taking advantage of Marie. It would have been all good if Marie was just using him for sex, but when she saw her friend getting in too deep, she didn't like it, especially since he had a girlfriend and he was selling her false dreams. It just sounded all too familiar to Lani and she tried to get her friend to see, but sometimes, someone can have you so open, you don't even see the bigger picture.

It was now the New Year. Lani couldn't believe it was 2002. She never thought she would live past seventeen and she didn't think anyone would live past the year 2000 for that matter. She kicked herself for not going to college. Nisha was in college doing her thing. She was in North Carolina attending Johnson C. Smith and majoring in Criminal Justice. With her good grades and smarts, Lani was supposed to be doing the same thing, rather than what she was doing back at home. Of the whole clique, Lani was the smartest. She was the one they came to for shit, and now she was the one wasting her talents and smarts to the streets.

She remembered putting in an application at an Applebee's Restaurant that was about to open. At the time she submitted the application, she was seventeen and she had to be eighteen to work in a restaurant which she turned a month later, but she never called back to follow up. She finally called in January and the manager remembered her. He set her up for an interview and she got the job. From then on, she was focused in a different kind of way.

A couple days later, however, she found out she was pregnant again. When she told Donell, he was happy and he wanted her to keep it. She was only eighteen and it was only a year since her last abortion, or rather her first. She decided to keep her baby and she was a bit excited. She liked Donell, but he didn't feel the same way about her. He liked her to a certain extent and he felt he should keep her around because he knew she could be different than what he was seeing on the surface. He also liked her because she knew how to ride the dick. She told Marie and Marie didn't really want her to keep it but the decision wasn't hers. Lani wondered how she would tell Lee that she was pregnant again. She decided to stall until her pregnancy became obvious.

At the rival basketball game between her alma mater and rival school, Marie and Lani had all eyes on them. No one knew Lani was pregnant at this time but Marie, Nisha and Donell. She was only about two months and her face was beginning to puff up. Everyone couldn't believe what they were seeing and they were the talk of the game. They had custom made baseball jerseys which they got made in the City with custom made fitted caps also done in the City.

Both their jerseys had the main men in their lives' street names (which everyone knew) on the back with however many numbers each hood represented. Marie had the number three for the "Tre" and Lani had the number four for the "Hill." On the hats, Marie had Torey's street name on one side and her name on the other side. Likewise, Lani had Donell's street name on one side and her name on the other. When Donell's ex-girlfriend seen that, she grabbed her friend and stared Lani down. She did not like what she was seeing, but if they were together, she did not stand her ground against Lani. Lani may not have had a tattoo repping her so-called man, but she repped him another way that was erasable.

Things were going pretty good in Lani's life. Donell was coming around more, telling her he couldn't wait for her to have the baby but a week and a half after she announced her pregnancy, he told her not to keep the baby. He told her he wasn't ready. Lani was lost. How could he go from being excited about the baby one minute to not wanting the baby at all? It just didn't add up but she didn't ask any questions, she just made her appointment that week without Lee even knowing and got rid of it. After she got rid of it, she still talked with him. He never really gave her an explanation as to why he wanted her to get rid of the baby, but he began acting strange.

One night when he came over, he started flipping on her telling her he wasn't really feeling her anymore because she was

95

messing around with T-Rizz. She was upset because she was being accused of something she didn't do and he was questioning her like he was her man. He was expressing anger as if he cared about her, but this was the same dude who told her he didn't feel the same way when she told him she loved him almost two months prior. So where was all the anger coming from? After they argued, he tried to have sex with her. It hadn't even been two weeks since the abortion and she wasn't even supposed to be having sex. She realized he didn't really care about her, he didn't want the baby but he didn't even use a condom. She lost interest in him after that night.

Chapter Eight: A New Love

Things began to get a bit chaotic in Lani's life. She hadn't talked to Donell in days and she didn't care. She was fed up with the bullshit and she vowed she would really be good on guys until she got her life together. She knew she hadn't really done anything to him so she knew he would get what he deserved.

After her decision to leave Donell alone for good, she went back to her old ways – hustlin'. Her new motto was *fuck niggas, get money*. She really meant what she said too (at the time), she was straight on guys. Over the next few weeks, she saw a lot of things change. She and her mother moved out of the house they were living in for over ten years. Though it was time to move since the house began to become shabby, she had a lot of memories (good and bad) at that house. They moved into her older cousin's apartment with her husband, as they waited for the apartment they were moving in to get finished. They were moving on the first floor of a house her cousin and her husband were buying so they were waiting for the house to get closed on. Not too long after that, Lani found out Donell was in jail.

Although she knew he would be getting what he deserved, she didn't think it would be so soon and she didn't really want him to be in jail. Ironically, he was in a police pursuit while he was in the car with T-Rizz. When they pulled over, everyone jumped out the car and started running. He was the only one caught and he was caught with drugs on him. After all he put her through, she still felt

97

the need to get in contact with him. She went on the internet and got his inmate number and address from the Connecticut Doc website. She wrote him and he wrote her back and attached a visiting form to the letter so she could start visiting him. This was the time Lani should have really shitted on him, but for some reason, she just couldn't let go.

She began visiting him which was not an inconvenience since he was within walking distance from where she lived and hung out. Things were going okay until her third visit when Donell started again with the bullshit. He told her she was playing him the whole time they were dealing with each other. He told her he heard she fucked two other dudes while they were together. For two people who never had a boyfriend-girlfriend relationship, they both acted like it. One of the dudes she never even heard of, and the other dude she fucked before she started dealing with Donell. Initially he did not believe her and he was cursing her out from behind the thick glass that separated them. He didn't start believing her until she started crying in the visiting room. That was the first time she let him see her cry; she really liked him.

After that visit, she didn't visit him for a while. She was upset. Most of her anger wasn't toward Donell, it was more toward the bum niggas in jail who had nothing better to do than sit around and hate on people. She was content though because she was honest and either he was going to accept that or not; so she resumed her normal activity.

She put her hoody back on, got her a bike and rode through different hoods selling her crack with no nigga on her mind – just money. A couple days later, she received a letter from Donell. His letter was very apologetic and he also expressed sympathy because he didn't realize she cared about him so much until she cried in the visit. He may have been running jail game but whatever the case, it was enough to get Lani to visit him again.

Between Donell stressing her out because she didn't know how he really felt about her and her living situation, things just weren't going right in her life. She didn't really stay home because she didn't have any privacy; to buy some time she worked and roamed the streets until all types of hours.

She still hustled, making a couple extra dollars aside from her paycheck. Most of the time, however, was spent with Marie. During this time, Lani and Marie became closer than ever. Lani even hung out at Marie's job. Because Marie's aunt and husband owned their own soul food restaurant, it worked out okay. Sandra's became a second home for Lani as she was there everyday, so they hung together more than ever.

After things became better with Donell, Lani started visiting him a lot more. After about five visits, however, she was not the only one visiting him. His ex-girlfriend, the one he was with since he was fifteen, started visiting him also. There were times when Lani and Solange were in the visiting room waiting to visit him at the same time. Since the inmates were allowed two visits a day, he was allowed to see both of them. He finally admitted to Lani that Solange was his girlfriend. He explained he only got back with her because he thought Lani played him with the two guys, especially since she didn't visit him for a while after that. He also told her they recently got back together right before he went to jail but ensured her "there are no relationships in jail." Although she was hurt once again, she didn't seem phased by the fact he was having his cake and eating it too. He probably felt like the man. Even through the taunting by Solange and a friend she started going to the visits with, who visited

Donell's older brother, Lani felt the need to stick by him and both females felt the same way.

After Big Lee found drugs in Lani's gym bag, Lani felt the need to leave the streets alone. After all, she was a female and she was not built for the streets. She was afraid to go to jail and she was afraid to get shot, so she definitely did not need to be there. Although Lani claimed she was holding the drugs for a friend, Big Lee was no idiot. She already previously heard Lani was hustling so the findings were confirmation. Lee was furious, especially since Lani had the drugs in someone else's house. Aside from that, Lee made the assumption everyone makes when they see a drug dealer – they're making money. She asked Lani how she could keep drugs in someone's home without contributing to bills. In her thoughts she answered, *I ain't making shit to give*, but verbally she did not respond. In Lani's usual reaction when she and her mother had disagreements, she didn't show her face for a few days.

She continued to visit Donell as each visit drew them closer than ever despite the fact he had another female seeing him conspicuously. He even told her he loved her. He told her he wished she would have kept the child they conceived. He apologized, explaining he asked her to get rid of the child because he felt like she wasn't fit enough to be a girlfriend, let alone a mother, and because he had gotten back with Solange and was trying to make it right with her. Those words hurt more than anything Donell ever did. She appreciated his honesty but she would have been better off not knowing his reasons for wanting the abortion. She began to think back to the basketball game when Solange noticed her with the jersey on, then two days later, Donell told her he didn't want the baby. She knew then that Solange must have approached him about the situation and he probably wanted to get back with her then so that was the reason he told her to get rid of the baby; had he gotten back with Solange and she found out he had a baby on the way, she wouldn't have been with him so he had to do what he had to do.   Though hurt, that still wasn't enough to keep her away from him. She had been through a lot with him and she just couldn't see he was no good for her and God had something better ahead.

The day Marie's brother, DaRon Shaw (he inherited his mother's last name), or Love, came home from a four year bid for assault with a deadly weapon, was the day Lani found out she had an older brother after nearly eight years of friendship. Although she heard Marie and her father mention it previously, it didn't dawn on her until she was face to face with Love, who was definitely Marie's father son. Love was light-skinned, standard height and medium build. He had that fresh jail glow to him being that he was fresh on the scene of things. His goatee made his face but the one thing that probably made Lani look the other way was that he wore a kufi hat. Like all brothers who go to jail and decide to turn Muslim, he kept his traditions. He even had the prostration mark in the middle of his forehead from making salat (or prayer in English). After Marie introduced the two, Lani moved on to a more interesting task. The next few weeks turned out to be very interesting.

Over the next few weeks, Love would often tell Marie he saw her friend (Lani). He would mainly ask what was wrong with her because he would see her listening to her CD player and dancing while walking down the street with her bookbag – which she kept with her as if she had an arsenal of weapons in it. Lani loved her music so it was very common for Marie to see and hear about what Love told her, but it was something he had never seen before. She would often listen to her music while on the bus going to work. She would rap her lyrics for everyone to hear without a care as to what they thought, often fantasizing about having her own car that she could listen to the music in. The music was her way of receiving advice no one else could give at the time. She loved R&B when she was sad, and she loved rap when she was happy. She appreciated a female or male who expressed themselves about relationships because it was her means of connecting with her own feelings.

When Marie told Lani about Love's inquiries (more than once), Lani began to think he may have a crush on her. "I'm telling you Marie, your brother like me. Why he keep telling you he saw me? Ain't nobody worried about somebody they don't know unless they like them." Lani would often say. Marie would just laugh.

Sure enough, after about a couple weeks, Love asked Marie for Lani's number. Lani wasn't interested in Love though. For one, she didn't think he was all that handsome because of the night she saw him with the kufi on and he was light-skinned. Lani only dealt with one light-skinned guy before and that was Mike; and he didn't make her decision any better with his "baby dick." She didn't really like light-skinned men, which probably stemmed from the bastard for a father who was never in her life. Marie knew this, yet she still gave the number.

When he first called, Lani's mother answered and she and Lani's cousin (the one they lived with) tried to figure out his age. From his deep, smooth voice, they thought he was about thirty years old. At the time he called, Lani and Marie just so happened to be on the phone.

"Okay, why did you give him my number?" Lani asked Marie.
"Because." Marie said laughing. "He just kept asking."
"You wrong, you wrong. I got you though."

"Just talk to him. Tell him you not interested yourself because I already told him. I even told him you had a boyfriend in jail. Obviously he doesn't care."

"Alright, I'm hanging up, I'll talk to you later." Lani hung up with Marie and accepted Love's call. At the time, she was eighteen, soon to be nineteen and he was twenty-two turning twenty-three two months after Lani. Although she wasn't attracted to him, she was impressed with his conversation. He wasn't like any of the other guys she dealt with in the past, at least not initially. The good, too, he wasn't a Leo, instead, he was a Libra and he didn't have any kids, which is always a plus.

From day one though, he expressed his interest in having kids, and he wanted them soon. Lani tried to warn him about the females and not to be so quick to run up in anything raw. She told him about the many diseases being passed and everyone was fucking everyone. He told Lani all about his four year bid. He expressed that it was the best thing that ever happened to him. It molded and shaped him into a man. He also said that was one place he did not want to go back to if he could help it. He told Lani his mother and two year old brother died from AIDS when he was fifteen years old; he was basically on his own. Here Lani was thinking she had it bad and this man lost his family. It's true, there's always someone in a worse situation than you.

In the neighborhood he grew up in, he had no choice but to turn to the streets. To lose a mother (pretty much his only parent because his father wasn't around as much as he should have been) at that age was devastating. Not only didn't he have his parent, but he had no one to provide for him, so he provided for himself. From his tone, Lani could tell he was still sad, and who wouldn't be. She expressed her sorrow to him but she could never match the feeling he felt.

Love had much of his father's ways. He told Lani stories about how his father did it big back in the eighty's and how he taught so many other dudes how to hustle. His father had a legacy on the streets, but the way he was at this time was not him at all. His father also had many women. He had about eleven kids by different women. He wasn't a bad father, but he wasn't the best either. Love expressed some resentment toward his father because he would lie to him when he was younger and tell him he would pick him up; Love would wait on the porch and his father would never show. He was too busy running the street so to show his love, he would provide for him financially. Lani could relate to the feeling he felt about this particular subject, but at least Love's father supported him financially and acknowledged him as being his child. Love was also stubborn like his father, and him losing his mother only made it worse. He became a loner and everything was his way or no way. He felt he didn't have to neither listen to anyone nor did he have to answer to anyone since he didn't have a mother.

Lani told him all about Donell and their situation. She told him about the other chick who was visiting him also. Ironically, Donell and Love were related on his father's side. They were first cousins, but they never spoke because they never really knew each other. His father's side of the family was extremely big and he had many cousins out there who he didn't know. Love didn't care about Lani's situation with Donell because he wasn't someone he was cool with. Family or not, they were strangers according to Love. He told her she didn't need to be with someone like that and she deserved better. She knew he was most likely telling her that because he wanted her, but at the same time it was true.

For the first time in her life, Lani believed there were good men out there. She enjoyed every bit of their conversation and looked forward to talking with Love again and she did. Over the next few days, she learned more and more about him, and he learned more about her. He was on parole until October (a couple days before his birthday) and lived with his aunt at the time. He had to get a job (which would be his first) if he wanted to get parole off his back; he definitely did not want to go back to the big house. He also expressed anger because he wasn't getting money like he used to.

When his mother died, he began selling drugs to satisfy his needs. Because he was so young and inexperienced, he sold bundles for the older dudes in his housing projects. He was from the "Jungle," which was across the street from the train station and in back of the police station. He was loyal to his hood. He made it clear that the "Jungle" set the foundation for hustling. According to him, "nobody saw money like the Jungle." He explained back then the money was coming. He was a worker (not even a boss) making three thousand a day, that's just how booming his housing projects were. Three thousand a day for a fifteen or sixteen year old, that was lovely, and that's what sucked him in. The streets were also the reason he shot someone. It was over drug turf and he was seventeen at the time. He said the boy did die for a few seconds but they brought him back to life and when he became alert, he told the police on Love. He was blissful the boy didn't die or he could be in jail doing life, which most of his friends he grew up with were already committed to. He told her about one of his best friends who he loved like no other who was incarcerated for a body. He wanted his friend to be out so bad because according to him, he was the only one on his level; he vowed he would help him the best way he could because that was just how real he was.

Lani was not at all intimidated by Love. She was attracted to bad boys who sold drugs and played with guns so he was no different. He was different though. He was a gangsta and a gentleman. He told Lani she shouldn't be out in the street at night just roaming because it was too dangerous in the street. Love recognized Lani was a ride or die chick. She was feeling him but she had it in her mind not to get serious with anyone again. Although he was a nice man, he was still a man and we know what that's about. Lani just didn't have any more room for hurt.

Over the next couple weeks, Love made an effort to get Lani to his aunt's house. He hadn't had sex in four years so she couldn't blame him for trying. She also started seeing him in the street often. The day she became attracted to him physically was the day she would change her life (not over night). She was chilling on her cousin's porch, which was about a mile from Love's grandmother's house. Love was riding his bike up the street when he saw Lani and stopped. He was bright yellow and his face was glowing like the Sun that shined the Earth. He had a fresh haircut minus the kufi hat, and a nicely trimmed goatee. His lips were bright red and he looked so blazin to Lani. Her cousin, M dot, just finished rolling the weed they went half on and purchased. She didn't want him to pass the weed in front of Love because she didn't want him to know she smoked, let alone see her smoke. They talked for a few and she couldn't help staring at him in which he returned the gesture. They both wanted each other and it was obvious.

"Here Lani." M dot said, passing the weed.

"What? You know I don't smoke." Lani replied.

"You don't smoke? When did this start? You just went half with me on this." He said in his Eddie Murphy tone of voice and laughed.

"Oh she did. She trying to front now." Love added, also laughing.

"Yeah she did."

"I didn't buy it for me to smoke, I just went half on it with you." Lani said laughing.

"Oh, okay, this all me then, thanks." Lani was upset because she did want to smoke, but she was willing to waste her money and weed so Love wouldn't see her smoke. By the time he left, the weed was gone but she didn't sweat it; she was on cloud nine in her own way. Later that night, she had to tell Marie how blazin her brother was looking.

"Yo, I saw your brother today, he was looking right." Lani proclaimed enthusiastically.

"Ohhhh, now you think he cute. You was shitting on him before." Marie replied laughing.

"I wasn't shitting on him, just that he wasn't that attractive to me."

"So what did he have on?"

"He didn't have nothing spectacular on, he was just shining in the face."

"So what does that mean?"

"Nah, it doesn't mean anything, I just wanted to tell you how sexy he was looking." Lani was definitely interested in Love after that, but she also didn't want to get involved with him. She didn't want to mess up the friendship she shared with Marie and she didn't want to get involved in another relationship because she thought she would get hurt again; besides, his whole family was players. His father had about eleven kids with multiple baby mothers and all his other uncles (four of them) had just as many. His cousin, Donell, was on the same boat as Lani experienced his shit first hand. She just wanted to be friends with him; possibly friends with benefits. It was strange though, because she kept saying she wasn't going to mess around with him because he was Marie's brother, yet she continued to talk to him.

Love showed Lani each day how different he was from any other dudes she dealt with. He would call her his African queen (something he probably adapted by becoming a Muslim) and many other beautiful names no one ever called her. Since he was a big fan of Nas, he probably adopted calling women "Queens" from Nas. What she didn't like though was some of the ways he thought. He believed the man was the king and the woman (the queen) should submit to the man. Basically, the woman should cater to the man's every need. She disagreed because she never did whatever a man asked, not even her father. That was probably the one thing that turned her off but she wasn't a woman yet, so she didn't understand what he was implying at the time.

The first time she went to Love's house was interesting. He no longer lived with his aunt at this time, instead he moved in with his grandmother. They talked for a few in the living room and then he invited her to his room. She stayed for a few before departing. He didn't even try anything on her and she respected that. She knew there was more to a relationship than sex and he only confirmed there were other guys out there who also knew. The more they talked, the more she gained feelings for him. He eventually turned back to the street for extra money because his paychecks just weren't enough for him. He wasn't out there heavy initially, but he was out there. When Lani got her new cell phone with a monthly bill, she gave her prepaid phone to Love. That was a reflection of her liking for him.

Although she liked him, he started to become aggravating. They had an argument one day that made her feel differently about him and they didn't talk for a couple of weeks. It didn't bother her either since didn't have any feelings for him and she didn't have sex with him. Eventually he came back around and Lani embraced him with open arms because everyone deserves a second chance (depending on the circumstance). This time around, he was in it for the long haul.

Things began to get a little more serious between the two. They spent a lot of time at his grandmother's house and there were numerous times when he tried to have sex with her. Half of the time she refused, while he refused the other half claiming he didn't want to take advantage of her. That may have been part of his game, but it was good game. It showed Lani she was worth the wait and it made her want him even more.

It was the day of Lani's birthday. She was having a get together at the Holiday Inn. Before she met Nisha and Marie she stopped by to see Love; he had a gift for her. He brought her some Timberland field boots with the army fatigue on the sides. She wasn't the type to accept gifts she didn't like. She would rather tell a person she didn't like it rather than keep the gift in the closet collecting dust. She told him she appreciated the thought but she didn't wear the boots; they weren't her style. She was being honest, but he didn't want to hear that. He was a bit embarrassed because Marie and Lani were laughing. He told her he would take them back and give her the money but he gave them to his little cousin and never got her anything. That was the first time a man brought her a gift, so she knew he was something special.

After Lani's get together was over, she had the hotel to herself. She had smoked and drank her nineteenth birthday away.

109

She called Love and tried to get him to the room. They would have a free room and privacy, but he didn't come. He told her he didn't want to take a cab there and he would see her the next day. That was very unusual and Lani wasn't used to that type of response. It was almost like he was the female and she was the dude. She had no choice but to accept his decision (although he did want to come) so she slept alone.

The next day, Marie, Lani, and Nisha were going to Times Square to chill and continue celebrating Lani's birthday. Before they departed, Lani went to see Love. She had to meet Nisha and Marie at the train station in an hour, so she had some time to buy. Usually Love would tease her and come close to hitting it and then stop, but today was different. Lani was always scared to have sex with him because he just seemed like he had a monster dick from when it poked her but that was just probably jail build-up flowing there. This time he took her pants off.

"You ready?" He asked in a seductive voice.

"Um huh." Lani replied more ready than ever. After waiting five months, she was going to give Love some. He strapped on the condom and put it on her. He wasn't at all rough either, as some other men on a drought would be. He was nice and gentle and they both climaxed. Lani fucked Marie's brother.

Over the next few weeks, Lani became more attached to Love. She started staying over his grandmother's house (even though she didn't approve of it because she was old school) and even had a drawer in his room with extra clothes. There was something special about Love. She never had a man like him in her short lived life, but she still didn't want to get serious. Unfortunately, she had no choice. Love made Lani look at life differently. She spent less time in the streets and more time with him. She became more focused on what was important in life. Over a three week period, she stacked $1200 of work money (she was a waitress). She got her driver's license a month after her birthday and brought a car right after that. She rushed to get a car so she got a piece of shit, but it was her first car and she loved it. She didn't register her car for a few weeks, she just threw a plate on it that she borrowed from a friend. She would bring Love to work in the morning and sometimes his friend too. Lee wasn't seeing her daughter for weeks at a time, but she never punished her daughter for that because Lani was grown now; she wasn't in high school anymore – she was free. All her mother asked of her was to pay four hundred dollars for rent once they moved into their new apartment.

Lani thought she was the shit when she got her car. Although it was an eighty-nine Honda Civic hatchback, she and Marie didn't have to walk anywhere ever again. They reminisced on the times they would be walking in the freezing cold and would say they couldn't wait to get a car. They fantasized about going this place and that place but once they actually had a car, they didn't really go anyway; they were just happy to know they had transportation when it was time to go places. Lani was just happy to have a car so she could listen to her stereo system.

Over time, things became more and more serious between Lani and Love. One night as she was bringing Love to a friend's house, she felt butterflies in her stomach for some reason. Love stepped out the car and left his cell phone in the car (the one she gave him). It rung and she answered it. She already knew she was his girlfriend because he told Marie she was, so she had every right to answer his phone. Besides, she was the one who gave him the phone.

"Hello." Lani answered.

"Uh yes, is Love there?" The female's voice on the other end asked. Lani's stomach dropped; she had been in this situation before with Kane.

"No, may I ask who's calling?" Lani didn't even get wild, she remained calm.

"Yes, Monica."

"Oh, okay well I'll tell him you called." When Love returned to the car, she went off on him. "Who the fuck is Monica?" She asked, handing him the phone.

"Monica?"

"Yes, Monica, she just called you."

"Oh, that's a basehead, I'm trying to work out her crib."

"Yeah whatever Yo." That was exactly the type of shit she did not want to go through which is why she wanted to be single but him being persistent and not respecting her needs, she returned to the bullshit. Love called Monica back to prove himself to her, but his plan backfired. Monica was questioning him about who Lani was.

"That was my wifey, what you mean who was that." Love asked shockingly. Lani couldn't hear what Monica was saying but he was not convincing. They drove back to Love's house and Lani was fumigated. He kept telling her the same thing but she wasn't listening. They relaxed in his room while Lani had a mean expression on her face. After silence for about five minutes, he began speaking. "Lani." She glanced over at him. "I am about to say something and I mean this from the bottom of my heart." Lani didn't know what he was about to say. She had been with him for eight months, well she knew him for eight months (they were friends first) but she was his girlfriend for about three, so she didn't know what to expect. "I Love You." He said sincerely. Lani was speechless. She never heard a man proclaim his love for a woman

112

first. She knew he was serious too because he was a grown ass man who didn't play those type of games. Secondly, she didn't know what to say because she didn't feel the same way. She was shocked so she just stared into his eyes for a few seconds and said it.

"I Love you too." She knew eventually she would grow to love him.

Chapter Nine: All Types of Problems

Lani felt guilty about telling Love she loved him and she didn't. She cared for him and he was special to her but she didn't love him at the time. He would tell her she was the woman he dreamed about in jail but she would tell him he didn't even know her when he was in jail. She never understood what he meant, but in all actuality, he was the man she always dreamed of too. All the songs she heard about the fairy tale relationships and love along those lines, she knew this had to be him. The crazy thing was, when he was incarcerated, he asked his sister to put him on with one of her friends. Marie told him she only had two friends, Nisha and Lani. So without even asking Lani, Marie gave him her address. He never wrote so she never knew about it until he told her. What was he thinking anyway, that Lani would write back and she didn't even know him or what he looked like; she didn't like writing letters anyway. She knew if she continued relations with Love she would grow to love him and if they stopped seeing each other, hey, she didn't love him so it would be nothing.

They did continue relations though. He was changing her slowly but surely. She always wore boy clothing and he was dying to see her in female clothing. She told him she wore boy clothing because that was what she felt comfortable wearing. She didn't see the point in walking the street in heels. That just looked crazy to her. She did dress like a female once in the blue and when she did, it made heads turn. Nisha and Marie also started seeing the transition

114

as well. The first time he saw her dressed up was on Christmas.
She went to his grandmother's and when he opened the door, he
was ecstatic. He couldn't believe how different she looked when she
dressed up. She looked so good to him he took her upstairs and
gave her a quicky, with everybody downstairs.

Lani was content with Love. She didn't know what their future
looked like, but for the time being, she knew it was good. She visited
Donell one last time to rub it in his face that he missed out on
something good. She made sure she looked right so she could hurt
him even more. She told him she had a new man and she wouldn't
be able to write or visit him anymore. Behind the glass he looked
hurt, but no telling what he was thinking inside. Whatever the case,
she felt good about what she had done because he deserved every
bit of it.

Love was back in the streets heavy now. He had quit his jobs
to pursue hustling full time. She was furious at that decision. She
didn't knock a dude who wanted to hustle, shit, it's hard enough
being black in America, it's even worse being a black male; but she
wanted him to be smart about it and quitting his jobs was not smart.
He started hanging with a few of his cousins from around Lani's
hood, one being Wayne, her junior high sweetheart. She didn't
approve of this either because those dudes were wild and Love
wasn't wild anymore, he just wanted money. His cousins liked to
shoot shit up and she didn't want Love involved in any bullshit, but he
was hard headed and he didn't listen.

He was making the money and he put his cousins down with
him. Back in the day he was the worker and now he was the boss
with his own workers. Lani watched him go from paycheck to a
couple thousand before her eyes. He was hustling hard. He let her
come on his first trip to New York since he been home. She was his

115

"murda mami." He shut the game down after that. He trusted Lani so he had her hold four thousand dollars at her house. She couldn't believe the kind of money he was making. In her small town that was a lot. All the dudes she dealt with were eight ball flippers. He had his own car that she registered because he didn't have any license and he was doing his thing for real.

Love was still stuck in the eighty's so his first car was an eighty nine Cadillac Seville. He loved Cadies, apple jack hats, Kangols, he even got parts in his hair. Only thing he was missing was the gold teeth. This was definitely new for Lani. He was a grown ass man who wore linen and gators.

He was also different because he would always ask Lani when he was going to meet her mother. Lani never introduced any of her male friends to her mother because she didn't think any of them were worthy enough which leads one to wonder if she felt that way, why did she deal with them? She didn't even know why but she did know that she wanted her mother to meet a good man who she would be with for a long time. So to make sure Love was that man, he waited until Thanksgiving to meet her.

Lee probably thought he was about thirty years old when she saw him for the first time. He had a pink button up shirt on with a panama hat during their first meeting. Lee didn't know anything about Love but she now knew who her daughter was with for weeks at a time. Over time she would learn more and more about him and knew he was good for her daughter.

After Lani's car was stolen and found on a street abandoned with her stereo system and radio gone, she realized just how real Love was. She and a few of her friends were at her house and were about to leave. It was winter time so Lani often started her car up, locked the door and waited in the house. This particular night her car wasn't in front of her house; it was within eye distance but no one was watching the car. When they came out, they only saw glass on the ground from the shattered window. She wasn't as upset as she should have been, but that was her car. She flagged a cop down and they assisted in the search of the car. They didn't find it until the next day, around the corner from her house. She didn't know what to do after that. She didn't have any more money for a car. She would have to start from square one again. She didn't want to go back to the bus either; she was too used to driving. After crying to Love, he told her to take a thousand dollars from the money she was holding for him and go buy a new car. Not too many guys would have done that for her, especially none of the losers she dealt with in the past. She found a car for fourteen hundred so she grabbed four hundred more. She purchased a 1990 Honda Accord which was the "in" car at the time so she thought she was doing it big.

She was in a financial snag at the time. She had to register the car and she had to pay her four hundred dollar rent. She borrowed more and more money from Love with every intention of returning it. She knew she had to return it quickly though before he asked for it. The only quick way she knew how to do that was to hustle. She teamed up with Marie and they got an ounce of weed. Since Lani had a car, they purchased a pre-paid phone and pursued their mission. Lani and Marie parked at places like the gas station, the 24 store and other places shouting "twenties of haze. Twenties of haze." They started gaining customers that way too. Before they knew it, the phone was booming. They were up to four ounces on their own but Love didn't think she would blow like that and he didn't like it. He didn't want her to get robbed or hurt, but he had no problem asking her to flip a thousand dollars for him. She knew if

117

she did that, she wouldn't have to use much of her own money to replace his money.

Lani had never had a man like Love. Love treated her like she should have been treated. He showed her how a real man treated a woman. Their sex life was great too. He was probably the first dude who represented the first time they had sex. Even right after that he started eating her pussy. Being the grown man he was, he wanted Lani to return the favor. He didn't ask her right away, but after pleasing her and she didn't do it on her own, he had no choice but to ask.

During one of their many sex acts, he kindly asked her to "kiss it." Lani didn't really want to do it because she never liked that. She thought that was so nasty. He asked her why she didn't want to do that to her "man." Since he put it that way and she trusted him, she sucked him off. It wasn't as bad as she thought and she did it good her first time. The only thing she didn't like was the pre-cum that went in her mouth; she hated the taste of it. She didn't understand what the big deal was and why people made it seem so difficult to do, but she was happy she did that to someone special. She knew he deserved it and she also knew he would not run around telling people about what she did. She didn't want Love to go anywhere else to get that, so she had to hold it down in the bed with him. From that point on, she knew she had him right where she wanted him.

Real recognize real and Love knew Lani was real. He couldn't understand why no other nigga kept her. If he didn't know she was real, he definitely knew when she went up top to cop some coke for him. She offered to get coke for him since she was going up top to get some weed. From the first time Love took her up top to establish his own coke connect, she decided to get haze from that same guy. She took the trip by herself and Love was paranoid. He

118

knew he shouldn't have sent her but he also wanted to test her loyalty. Lani on the other hand, did not want him to get another female to take City trips with him because she didn't want him having female friends at all so she played every part she could in their relationship. She was on the train with a bunch of drugs and she didn't have any fear about it. As she always heard, "fear will get you caught." After that, Love did not want her to do that ever again, but he now knew what limits she was willing to go to.

Since business was booming, she was a little cocky. She hadn't been in her old hood much since she started dealing with Love, so she hopped out one day to show off. She parked her car out of sight. There was a dice game going on and she loved cee-lo. She started gambling and was taking the guys' money. She stopped when the cops were coming. While she was gambling, her money phone was ringing off the hook. Since she was winning at the dice game, she ignored the calls until the cops came and she decided to go serve her clientele.

When she got into her car, she noticed the portable DVD player that she and Nisha went half on was gone. She checked the back seat but it was not there. She also left an ounce of weed under the driver's seat. Lee was home so she didn't have time to bag it individually and instead took the whole ounce out the house. She reached behind her seat but there was no weed. She began to panic now. She didn't see any sign of forced entry so she didn't think anyone robbed her. She checked the trunk, but there was neither weed, nor the TV. She did notice that she left her passenger side window cracked. She knew there was no other possibility than robbery.

She knew Love would be upset. His money was tied into it and he always warned her that the dudes in her hood didn't give a

119

shit about her but she would always say the niggas were her niggas. This proved Love was right. Lani told D-Man what happened but he didn't care, he only told the other dudes. She felt the need to tell Marie since her money was involved also. She went to Marie's job and told her what happened. After she left her job, she went and sat in her car around the way, hoping to get information. As she sat in the car talking to D-Man, Love rolled up with his cousins in the car. "Yeah, I see you got robbed. And these your niggas. I told you. And you still over here, in niggas faces. You a stupid ass bitch." Whoa! That came from left field. Love never embarrassed her like that, let alone disrespected her like that. She felt small and she knew he was most likely showing off because he would have never said that to her had they been alone. She just wanted to go home and cry, but before she could, he blurted out, "And I'm straight too." Not only did he disrespect her, but he broke up with her also. Was he trying to show off? If he was, that was childish and she thought he was a man.

Instead of going home, she went back to Marie's job to tell her what happened, but Love beat her there. Upon arrival, he asked her to go to her house and get his money. "No, you not getting nothing." Lani said.

"No? It's my money. Don't play with me." Love said angrily.

"No, you tried to play me and you disrespected me. Take it as a loss nigga." Love laughed on the outside but he was heated inside. He went back in the restaurant and told Marie to tell Lani to give him his money. Lani wasn't bulging though.

"Fuck it, keep it. I'm good on you." Love said, walking away. Lani was sad and confused. She got robbed so why was he breaking up with her. She thought he was bluffing and he would eventually come around, but after not hearing from him for two days, she knew he was serious. That's when she realized she loved him. That's why they say you never miss a good thing until it leaves you. That's when Lani did something she never thought she would – got in stalker mode. She had to get Love back and show him she was sorry for whatever she did. And that she did.

For the next couple of days, she rode by everywhere he was and waited in front of his grandmother's house, but he showed no interest. She was never a morning person, something she adapted after high school, but one morning she called him at seven a.m. and told him to come downstairs and get his CD's. Seven a.m. to get CD's, that was a good way to get someone back. Love went to talk to Lani though. She handed him a letter she wrote and also had a conversation with him. She poured her heart out to him verbally and in the letter. It must have worked because they were back together. It was neither the letter nor the conversation that got them back together, but rather his feelings towards her. He really did love her.

He came over that night and everything seemed all good until the morning when he asked for his money. She didn't know what to do. She got the money for him and when he saw there was only two thousand dollars instead of four, he could have slapped her. He had worked hard for that money and he had told her stories about his family who got him for money. Aside from that, he was from the street and you could get killed for shit like that regardless of how much money it was; you would get blasted just on principal. Just like that, they broke up again.

Lani didn't know how she would get him back this time so she just did what came to her mind. She popped up at his grandmother's house and his grandmother let her in. She was in with the family at this time and he was in with hers. She went upstairs to his bedroom and had a talk with him. She really loved him and it took for

121

something bad to happen for her to know it. She remembered all the stories he told her about his family messing his money up and he forgave them. So what if they were family. She told him he should give her another chance too. She had already waited a week and he missed her just as much as she missed him, so he gave in again. She vowed to never do anything that would jeopardize their relationship.

Things did get back to normal between Love and Lani. She was losing Marie though. Marie met a new man since Torey was in jail again and she was lonely. She had ended affairs with Reno after realizing she would never be anything but a piece of ass and began seeing a dude named Mark. Ironically, Mark was Candy's (D-Man's girlfriend) baby's father. At this time though, D-Man was locked up. Candy, Marie, and Lani were cool because of D-Man. They weren't best friends, but they chilled occasionally.

Mark was handsome. He was getting a little money too. Marie liked Mark, but she didn't want him to know. Mark was cocky and conceited. He also fucked a lot of girls. He wasn't the love them and leave them type, more like the fuck them and leave them type. His only serious relationship was with his baby's mother, Candy. It was also rumored he had another baby but he wasn't sure if it was his. He cheated on his baby mother often and once she got fed up, she felt she should get even, so she fucked his friend. He was a man of pride, so he couldn't let that slide.

Mark was a cool dude in Lani and Marie's eyes. He also seemed like he had money. He had a brand new 1997 Acura Integra straight off the lot. It was shiny black with shiny chrome rims and complimented by smooth black leather. The best thing Lani liked about the car was his booming stereo system that was powerful enough to pop someone's eardrums; she loved that type of system because it made the music sound like a club. Mark was the type of guy who thought he knew everything and you couldn't tell him he was wrong. He made it clear that he thought every woman was shiesty. He just didn't trust females and always thought they were up to something. He made it clear that those were his reasons for being the way he was. He didn't want any girl to get near his heart again.

As Lani talked with him one day by herself, she assured him she had a good man and that her man wasn't cheating. Mark burst her bubble by telling her all men cheat. "Some do it all the time, some do it once in the blue, but all men cheat no matter what you think," he assured her. "He may not be cheating on you now, but he either did before or he will." After that, Lani knew something wasn't right with him. She stood her ground and he didn't know her man so she didn't listen to him. It was weird to her because he was saying that to her, but yet he added that he wasn't like that. Well he was a man so what was really good?

Now Marie was with him. They were just friends at first. Nothing went on with them because Marie always dragged Lani along when they chilled. Lani had her own man she had to cater to though, so she didn't hang with them all the time. Eventually Marie and Mark had sex. Marie didn't tell Lani right away because friends don't tell each other everything and that's a true fact no matter what you think. And they don't have to either, it's their business, nobody needs to know. She did tell Nisha though. Nisha was away at school in North Carolina since they graduated which resulted in her never being around.

When Marie finally told Lani, she also told Lani she was hooked. Mark had put it on her. "He got the magic stick," were her exact words. She gave Lani specific details about their sex life and told Lani he was her best sex partner thus far. The descriptions Marie gave Lani made Lani create a vivid image in her head. Though she would never cross her friend like that, it's only natural for human beings to imagine how a person fucks when they're hearing what they do in bed. That contributes to about ninety percent of the reason why friends sleep with their friends' man – they want to see for themselves just how good it is, which is why "every little thing that we do, should be between me and you." It started out as a sexual relationship but Mark gained feelings for her. It came to the point where he wanted Marie to tell Torey she didn't want to be with him anymore; hell, he was cheating on her anyway from jail. Eventually she did break it off with Torey and was with Mark. Mark did things for her that Torey would have never done, so she didn't lose out on anything. All men are dogs, but wouldn't you rather have one who looks out for you rather than a give you hard dick and bubble gum? Lani and Marie were still visiting Candy also, despite Marie's dealings with her baby's father.

Love had a thing with his sister fucking niggas. Although she was grown and had been having sex before he came home, he just didn't like to know his little sister was having sex. He always wanted to protect her and encouraged her to mess with a dude who was worth something. Mark had an issue with a few dudes from his projects. The issue supposedly stemmed from money and drugs. There are always two sides to a story and from what Lani and Marie heard, Mark got his childhood friend for $10,000. Mark defended himself, but it all boiled down to money and drugs. His friend had it out for him and he wanted to kill Mark. When Mark was spotted on New Haven's busiest strip, Whalley Ave., his friend started shooting at him. Mark was able to get away from them but they shot his back window out. Luckily Marie wasn't in the car, but when Love heard the news of that, he was fumigated. He had a mission to end their relationship from that point on.

On his way to the "Jungle" one day, Love spotted Mark on one of his friends' porch. Initially he wanted to go get his cousins so they could beat his ass, but then he wanted to handle it on his own. He pulled over and got out the car. As he walked over to him, Mark extended his hand as if to give him dap. Love quickly slapped his hand away and said, "Don't fucking give me dap. We ain't cool. What the fuck is good with you getting shot at. You be having my sister in the car with you and you not gon' have her around that bullshit. If anything happen to my sister yo, I swear to God..." Mark didn't know what was going on.

"Naw yo, naw yo, it ain't like that man. I wouldn't have her in the car with me if that shit was happening." He quickly pleaded. Mark saw the anger in Love's eye and he didn't want to test him.

"Yo, I swear man, you stay the fuck away from my sister or it's gon' get ugly B. You gon' make me take it back to my old days." Mark's friend just stood in the doorway as if he knew Love meant business about his shit. He was a bad motherfucker in his time from what he heard and he wanted no part in what was going on between Mark and Love.

"Naw yo, chill chill. It ain't like that." Mark had his hands up now. Love wanted to punch him, but when he saw just how much of a pussy he was, he left it alone.

"Yo, stay away from my sister man, I ain't playing with you." Love walked away and Mark called Marie to break it off. He picked her up for the last time to tell her about what happened. On his way dropping her off, they rode past Love and Mark made her duck down. He did not want him to see that after he just told him what the consequences would be hours earlier. When Lani saw Marie that same day, she already knew what happened from her boyfriend. Marie expressed her sadness and anger for her brother doing what he did. She seeked Lani's advice and Lani told her to do whatever she wanted. Marie talked Mark out of breaking their relationship off, and they resumed seeing each other inconspicuously. After a while, Love knew they were still together, but he just let it be. He tried to protect his sister and she didn't listen, so he felt, whatever happens to her, it would be on her.

Candy and Mark hated each other, or so they said. They really didn't deal with each other from what Lani and Marie saw. Mark claimed he hated her because she called the cops on him (all men say that's the worst thing a female could ever do to them). Candy claimed she hated him because he didn't take care of his son but her hatred against him probably stemmed from all the wrongdoing he did in the past. He wanted to take care of his son he just didn't want her to be involved. There were times when Mark had Lani and Marie pick his son up and bring him to where he was. He didn't even want Candy knowing where he lived.

While Marie and Mark were getting serious, Lani had other things going on. She missed her period which sparked her to take a pregnancy test. She was pregnant again; she showed Love the pregnancy test and he was happy. Since he came home from jail, he wanted a baby. He wanted to fill the emptiness he had from losing his mother and little brother, so he was happy he would be having a little one. Lani didn't mind either. She would be turning twenty in a few months, she wasn't in high school anymore and the baby would have both parents. She was excited and she was not about to have another abortion, whether the dude wanted it or not. Although she had some freedom from her mother, she still didn't know how to tell her she was pregnant and she didn't tell her either.

About two months into the pregnancy, Lani began to have crazy, sharp pains. The pain began to become so severe that she couldn't stand up straight. She was also bleeding heavy. It was so severe that she thought she would pass out and die. She had become light-headed and no one was there with her. The pain subsided after a few days.

The pregnancy came at a bad time, however. She had crashed her car so she didn't have a car to get to where she needed to go. Love eventually got the car fixed but she waited a few weeks. It was his way of teaching her to stack her money. She was pregnant so she was constantly hungry. Since she didn't have transportation, she expected her baby's father to bring her whatever she wanted and wherever she needed to go. She called him one night and asked him to bring her a sub. She was appalled when he told her "No," he was busy getting money. The nerve of him; she was carrying his child and he was going to let them starve. She began to look at Love differently and she would never forget that because anytime he needed something, she dropped what she was doing and catered to him. She couldn't even borrow the car she registered to handle things she had to handle. She couldn't stand the fact that he let his cousins hold the car everyday instead of her.

Lani was still having sharp pains and bleeding. One night, she and Love were having sex and she stopped him because the pain was so severe. She couldn't stand up or move so Love made her go to the hospital. They waited in the emergency room for hours and never got called; they went back home and would return the next morning. When they went back the next day, Lani waited nine hours to find out she was had an ectopic pregnancy. The baby was developing in her fallopian tube and had to be removed. Her fallopian tube ruptured, causing that to be removed also. She could have died had she waited longer. Since she didn't have any insurance, she used a fake name so she wouldn't have to pay the high surgery bill.

The loss of the baby was devastating to both Love and Lani. Lani believed that was God paying her back for her abortions. She would be on bed rest for the next six weeks. When she returned home, she told Lee what happened and told her she didn't tell her she was in the hospital because she used a fake name. Lee told Lani she didn't think she should have children because she may think she know a man until kids come into play and the female wind up stuck, but she was only saying that because she didn't know what type of guy Love was; she thought he was a knucklehead.

The whole time Lani was on bed rest, Marie seen her once. The rest of the time she was with Mark. Lani resented her for that because she wasn't there for her like a friend should have been. She would lie to her and tell her she'd come by but never show up and she wouldn't answer the phone when Lani called. That was a lonely six weeks for Lani.

After she got better, it was the same thing from Marie, it seemed as if Mark was the only one who existed to her and Lani started to hate Mark because of that. It wasn't the first time Marie put a nigga before Lani and Lani resented her for that because she felt she would be there in the end when she wasn't with the nigga. Lani chilled with Candy a little more, but all she wanted to talk about was Mark. Lani didn't want to hear that, especially since she could hear it from Marie; Lani thought Candy was cool, that is until shit hit the fan.

Chapter Ten: Real recognize Real?

Marie and Mark became an item at this time and she would often stay the night with him (he had his own apartment). Although Mark and Candy hated each other, Candy did call him sporadically to talk to him about their son. One night, while Mark and Marie were together, Candy called at about one in the morning. Mark didn't have intentions on answering the phone but Marie advised him, stating it could be an emergency with his son. Mark answered and let Marie listen. The call was not about his son; she wanted to chat with him. For two people who hated each other, why did she want to chat? Marie did not like that at all because she felt violated even though Candy did not know about them. Calling someone at one in the morning usually meant a booty call. Regardless of the fact that she was his baby's mother, he was her man now so the only conversation she should have been trying to have should have involved his son. Since Candy was still with D-Man and D-Man was Marie's cousin, she decided to tell him about his girlfriend. Since he called her just about every night, her telling him came two days after the incident.

D-Man told Marie he wouldn't mention her name, but everyone knows that usually doesn't happen. D-Man asked Candy about calling her baby's father at one in the morning. Candy flipped on him and demanded to know who told him that. Initially D-Man told Candy his cousin told him. Coincidently, Mark talked to one of D-Man's cousins years ago so Candy automatically assumed it was her. D-Man went along with it until Candy began saying she would approach his cousin about it. That's when he told it was Marie because he didn't want his cousin to whip Candy's ass about some shit she didn't even know about; bad enough they already had a beef with each other. That confirmed Candy's previous assumptions that Marie was sleeping with her baby's father and still in her face. After she hung up with D-Man, she called Marie. Marie was on the phone with Lani at the time so she didn't answer. Instead, she [Marie] wanted Lani to call and see what she had to say. Lani asked Marie if she wanted to listen in secretly but she declined.

When Lani talked with Candy, Candy was furious. She claimed she was angrier because she lost a friend, but that was bullshit. She was mad somebody she knew was fucking her baby's father. Lani didn't tell Candy anything she didn't know already; she only confirmed things. Her only mistake was still being cool with Candy after that conversation.

Candy used Lani for a couple days until she started twisting Lani's words. That caused conflict between them because Marie thought Lani was talking about her to Candy. It didn't help either, that Marie had family in her ear painting a bad picture about Lani, and it didn't help that they thought she was a bad person anyway. It also didn't help that Marie also had Mark in her ear trying to convince her Lani wasn't right for still associating with Candy. Since he thought he knew everything, it was logical that he would put some shit in her ear about Lani that would seem believable. Their relationship was basically down the drain from then on; no matter how hard they tried, it just wouldn't be the same.

Lani tried to convince Marie to believe she didn't betray her. They spoke again but their friendship just wasn't the same. Lani ultimately decided she would leave their friendship in the hands of the Lord. She thought as long as she was with Marie's brother, they would always be cool, and she left it at that.

Lani and Marie didn't chat as much and they had a beef for about two weeks after the incident. After a get together at Humphrey's, Marie and Lani didn't even talk to each other. That was eating Lani up inside and it seemed as if Marie didn't even care about what was going on between them. After everyone went home, Lani decided to confront Marie about what was going on. At this time, Mark lived with his father again and since she knew where he lived, she went to the building and began yelling their names since she didn't know exactly what apartment they were in. She was drunk and she was not leaving until she got what she wanted to get off her chest.

When they finally came out, Lani was crying. She told her friend how she felt about the whole situation, but it was as if they were double teaming her; what she was saying was to no avail. Lani told Marie that Mark wasn't shit and all he wanted to do was get her pregnant and bounce on her like all the other females. Marie disregarded that comment and told Lani she was not getting pregnant. After the meeting, Marie and Lani spoke again and slowly it got back to how it used to be; but it still would never be the same.

Marie stayed to herself with Mark most of the time, growing their relationship. He began to catch deep feelings for her and that's when his true colors began to surface. Mark was a jealous motherfucker. Marie did pop up pregnant as Lani previously warned and Mark wanted her to keep the baby. She decided she would, but then she thought he would leave her to handle the responsibility by herself; so she got another abortion. She couldn't live with being a single parent and she vowed that if she ever had a baby by a dude and he left her on her own to raise it, she would leave the baby on the father's doorstep and disappear; let him see how it is to raise a baby on his own.

Every little thing Marie did, he accused her of cheating. They would argue about every little thing, even if it wasn't a problem of their own. He was the type of jealous that if she said something like *Jimmy got shot in the parking lot,* he would ask who the fuck Jimmy was, did she fuck with him; she literally had to watch everything she said and did. He just thought he knew everything and when he thought he was right, there wasn't anything one could do to change his mind. Marie's mother had a son who was about two years old at this time. Mark's jealousy was so out of control that he had it in his mind that the young boy was Marie's son. He told her the baby was Torey's son that they conceived together and she gave him to her mother to take care of him. Now that shit is crazy, no one should be that possessive. The little time Marie and Lani did talk, Marie would tell Lani about his abusiveness. Marie had been in an abusive relationship before, so this was nothing new to her; it just wasn't this extreme though. She would mistake it for love, and that was not the thing to do.

There was a time when he banged her head up against the car window, threw her out a moving vehicle, then pulled her by her hair and dragged her back in the car because he thought she was cheating on him. There was also a time when Lani really thought he would kill her. She accidentally called him Reno while they were at her aunt's house and he went sick. He pulled her out the house saying he wanted to talk to her and he took her in the backyard and began yelling at her while she was crying. Her aunt called her phone to make sure she was okay and somehow he answered unintentionally. Her aunt heard him yelling at her and heard him say he was taking her to his cousin's backyard so he could whoop her ass. Marie was scared and luckily her aunt heard everything or she could have gotten seriously hurt. Her aunt called back and told him she heard everything and if he put his hands on her she would "fuck him up," and she meant it. He damn sure didn't put his hands on her, but Marie still didn't leave.

Deshawn was very close to Marie; she called him her Godbrother. They had known each other before middle school and always remained close. He was also close with Lani and Nisha but he and Marie really had a brother and sister type of bond. When he got out of jail he would often visit Marie and call her just to chat. Mark didn't like it not one bit, always telling her that there were no such thing as a man and a woman being friends. But once again he was contradicting himself because he had a so-called best friend who was a girlfriend, so was he fucking her? He would accuse them of fucking and would often beat her ass whenever Deshawn called her. Marie and Nisha couldn't believe how he would act because Marie really wasn't fucking Deshawn. Lani would be so mad that Mark was beating on her and it was killing her not to tell Love, but Marie didn't want her to tell him. She told Lani to wait to tell Love until they broke up so he could get at him then when she wouldn't care. Lani had a gut feeling that one day he would kill her, and if he did, Love would kill him. She promised not to tell Love, but told Marie if she saw it with her own eyes she would tell him and wouldn't care how she felt.

Lani witnessed Mark's rage first hand which reminded her of Marky Mark's character from the movie *Fear*. While she, Mark and Marie were chilling in the basement of Marie's house, Lani was on Marie's cellphone talking to Nisha. While in her conversation, the phone rung and Lani looked at the phone. The name on the phone was Deshawn. Lani thought he was so aggravating and being that she was on the phone with Nisha, she didn't answer because he wasn't important enough for Lani to answer; besides, she didn't want her friend to get in trouble later on when she left. When she hung up the phone, Mark asked her to see the phone. Not thinking that he was mad and had peeped her look at the phone and didn't answer, he checked the call log and saw that it was Deshawn who called. He didn't say anything right away and they continued their evening until five minutes later.

"Yo, why you didn't answer when homeboy called?" Mark asked Lani angrily.

"Excuse me."

"Why you didn't answer when homeboy called?"

"Oh Deshawn? Dag, how you know he called?" Lani asked with a smile. "I didn't answer cuz I was on the phone and he is not that important."

"Yeah whatever, ya'll both wild."

"Who is wild yo, what are you talking about?"

"Yo, that nigga do not call you and Nisha at 10:30 at night. Why the fuck he always calling my girl?"

"First of all, he don't call me like that cuz we not all that cool. And when he did call me late before, my man did not have a problem with it. *Cuz he is not insecure, and he know nobody don't want no damn Shawn. Psycho ass,* Lani thought.

"That nigga wanna fuck my girl yo. I ain't havin' that shit." Marie just looked on as she was filled with anger. She was fed up with getting accused of doing shit she was not doing. Mark called Deshawn and told him he wanted to have a talk with him. On his way out, Lani decided to go with him to try to talk to him.

During their ride, she convinced him the best she could that nothing was going on between them two. Being who he was and how he thought, it only made sense that he didn't believe her because she was Marie's friend. He wanted to get his gun and go where Deshawn was waiting for him at. He was ready to fight him and whatever because he felt disrespected. After Lani calmed him down and did her best to convince him she wasn't cheating on him, he did not meet Deshawn and he left it alone. From that incident, Lani knew just how crazy the motherfucker could get; but the thing that got her so mad was the fact that he was not really the hard core nigga he portrayed and he would not beat on no nigga the way he did Marie.

While the beef between Marie and Candy was getting thick, Lani was making friends elsewhere. Out of the blue she became tight with a female from her job. Shaniya Jones, or Niya for short, was totally different from Lani. She was more of a white girl and she knew nothing about the streets but somehow they clicked. They immediately put their trust in each other and began telling one another their business. The reason they probably clicked was because they had similar situations. Like Lani, Niya had a best friend she wasn't on good terms with because she felt her friend put a man before her. Shit, her situation was a bit worse because her friend's man pulled a gun out on her and other friends; her friend did not do anything and of course she stayed with him.

Niya became Lani's new best friend. They partied, talked on the phone and hung out. Once Lani and Marie became tight again, Marie did not like that Lani had a new friend. Marie felt Nisha and herself should have been Lani's only friends. According to Marie, Lani shouldn't involve other "bitches" in their circle because "they didn't rock with other bitches." Lani didn't care though. That was the person she could go to when Marie wasn't available.

135

Marie would always say things like, "you don't know that chick, you can't trust her." Lani would just laugh and shrug Marie's comments off. But Marie wasn't the only one saying it; Love said it also. He told Lani she shouldn't be so quick to put her trust in the girl, he said "for all you know, she could be the police." That was probably him being paranoid because he was heavy in the streets.

Lani always wanted her own apartment. She felt that way ever since her mother began making her pay four hundred dollars for rent; she felt she could pay that in her own spot. The last draw was when she realized she didn't have any privacy. There was a blizzard one night, like ten inches of snow. Love wanted to see his "booby," as he would call her, and took a cab to her house because his car was in the shop. He chilled with her until late in the night. He tried to get a cab home but the snow was so bad, they were only transporting to the hospital so he fell asleep at her house. This was the first time her mother knew of him staying the night. When Lani got up in the middle of the night, Lee asked her if her "friend" was still there. She told her "yeah." Lee was mad and told her to keep the door open. She was embarrassed and Love was uncomfortable and couldn't wait to leave. He left as soon as the morning came.

The next morning Lee explained to Lani she didn't condone men staying the night. Lani felt she was old enough and she was paying four hundred dollars for rent. If age wasn't a valid reason, money should have been. Her opinions were conflicting with her mother's, so she felt best to move out. After that night, Lani and Love agreed to get their own spot since his grandmother was the same way. They shared their first apartment together.

Their first apartment wasn't all that great, but it was theirs. Love changed Lani and made her into more of a woman. Before him, Lani never cooked a meal; she didn't even know how to cook.

Once they moved in together, she made it her business to learn how to cook. She didn't want her man going anywhere else for anything, not even a meal. Moving out her mother's house was probably the best thing for Lani and her mom because they became tighter than ever; she became more open with her mom.

Lani and Love became closer than ever also. Living together was probably good for their relationship equally as it was with Lani and her mother. He spoiled her to death, showering her with all type of gifts. They argued here and there, but what couple doesn't? Marie would always get on Lani because her arguments with Love would be about dumb shit, while she was arguing with Mark about baby mothers. After an argument one night and he called her childish, she turned elsewhere for love because she didn't feel he loved her.

After not talking to him for about two years, Lani started visiting Donell again. She hadn't talked to him since her last visit when she told him she became serious with Love. Donell knew about Love and expressed his disappointment. He told Lani he was sorry for messing up and he wanted to be with her. Lani told him she was in love and she didn't think that would be possible (but if that was the case, why was she there). She only planned on visiting Donell to get back at Love for what he said but she became attached to Donell again and that made her confused. She still had feelings for Donell but she knew he would never treat her as well as Love did and she didn't want to go backwards. She also did not want to deal with someone who was in and out of jail.

She and Donell stayed in contact after the first visit. They wrote letters back and forth and she visited him a couple more times after. She was starting to fall for Donell again. He was probably running game on her or trying to use her since he knew she was doing well. He wasn't with Solange anymore after she moved on also and had a baby; because of that, he **suddenly** wanted Lani and she was the best thing that happened to him.

Slowly but surely Donell was wheeling Lani back into his life. She hated not knowing if he was real in what he was saying, but she believed everything he told her. He would assure her that he could show her better than he could tell her and he would make it is business to do just that when he touched ground. He shared things with Lani she always felt but didn't know. In particular, he told her he was out in the world wildin' out, fucking bitches on the regular which is why he never wanted a girlfriend. He told her he was out there with his head cut off. He told her he was a changed man and he was ready to settle down. Though Lani was disgusted, she still felt him. He told her he loved her and he was happy she changed. He ran all types of game on Lani and had her head fucked up once again. She had to realize what the hell she was doing and snap back into reality.

They say whatever is in the dark shall come to light. Never underestimate that saying because it is true. Lani was at work on her way out the door when Love called her. "When you coming home." Love asked.

"I'm about to leave now." Lani replied.

"Alright, well I have to talk to you. I can't be going through this."

"Going through what, what happened?"

"I'll talk to you when you get here. I need to talk to you face to face." Lani was nervous. Her stomach dropped. She didn't know what happened. She never cheated on him sexually so she didn't know what was going on.

When she arrived home, she didn't know what to say. The letters Donell wrote her were on the bed. Since Love never wrote or

138

used school items, she thought keeping the letters in a duffel bag with other stationery items was a good hiding place. It just so happened that this particular day Love needed paper so he could write his friend in jail. When he opened the duffel bag, he stumbled upon the letters and read all of them. Lani was receiving letters from an ex to the house she shared with her man.

Love felt disrespected for that reason, but he was more hurt at the contents of the letters. In one of the letters, Donell mentioned the visit so Love knew Lani visited him. Donell was also telling Lani he loved her in the letters. She never had a problem with Love cheating. If he was, she never heard about it. Although she didn't cheat, she violated. Love was through with her and she didn't think there was any hope then. He left out the door and she just sat crying. She needed a way to get him back to the house so she could talk with him, so she called Marie. She threatened to kill herself and even though she felt that way deep down inside, she couldn't do it. She knew Marie would tell Love and if he loved her, he would be there with the speed. Marie also knew Love had a gun in their house and she knew how much Lani loved him, so she was scared. As she knew he would, Love did rush back to the house. They talked, Lani apologized and he took her back. He wasn't over it though.

The next day, he went to Lani's mother and told her the situation. He even cried. He really, truly, genuinely loved Lani. Lani's mother flipped on her and told her she was wrong. She [Lani] was upset he even involved her mother. She did not need to know that and she did not need her mother to know she said she would kill herself. Her mother always told her about herself if she was wrong and Lani did not want to hear that. She didn't even know guys did things like go talk to the mother of their significant other.

She wrote Donell one final letter and told him she couldn't deal with him anymore. She didn't want to lose Love and she knew Donell wasn't going to change. He would not be a fair trade off if she lost Love. In his final letter, he vowed Lani would be his when he came home; he didn't care what he had to do.

Things got better with Lani and Love. At the same time, Lani and Niya were getting closer also. She only knew her a few months and she had been more of a friend than Nisha and Marie together. She was there for Lani when she needed her; she looked up to Lani like a big sister and Lani embraced her like a younger one. They were almost inseparable.

As Love became heavier in the street, Lani received more and more gifts. He would bring her flowers to work or have them delivered and he brought her whatever she wanted. He also began to get cocky and arrogant. Along with the gifts also came fear. She knew there was only two ways the drug game ended, by death or jail so Lani wanted him to stop. She was probably more afraid of the jealous dudes in the street than the police. Where she was from, she didn't know too many dudes getting money like Love. He had a six thousand dollar rose gold chain with his projects, the "Jungle," as the medallion with clear and black diamonds to accentuate the distinguished piece on his neck and he made it his business to stay fly. He made the investment in his chain when he got his first half a bird. All it would take was for a robbery to go bad and it would go bad because Love promised if he ever got robbed, he wasn't giving nothing up – he would fight for the gun. Because of his mentality about that subject, she feared something would happen to him and she was too attached to him to deal with that.

Love had been in the streets since months after he came home from jail. Up to this point (two years into the game), he hadn't run into the police. But as we know, all things must come to an end eventually.

Since business was booming, Love began to get cocky. He was making the money and he had a good girl on his side. He praised Lani for sticking by him and told her if it wasn't for her, he would have never gotten as far as he was in the game. He had a decent amount of money, but people on the outside looking in thought he had much more than he did. To Love, all other guys were "bums" compared to him. He felt himself more than anything else and he thought he couldn't be touched. Though Lani didn't like how he was changing, she didn't forget the sweetheart she knew he could be. Love would send Lani flowers to her job with poems attached. That would always make her blush because her co-workers would say "ooh" and tell her what a good man she had.

Lani also didn't like how kindhearted Love was. She didn't want anyone mistaking his kindness for weakness because in the end, he would be the one assed out. He put his family members down with him and they would often fuck up his money and he would take a big loss, often resulting in him not being able to come up and get to the point he wanted to be. This affected Lani more than him because she wanted him to hurry up and get what he needed and get out the game. His goal was $100,000 and he would open up some businesses and quit for good. Besides, if she couldn't be the one fucking up his money, she didn't want anyone else to.

After Mark was pulled over in Hamden and had no driver's license, he was arrested for assault on a police officer. At this time, it became evident that he really didn't have as much money as previously thought; he couldn't even post a $2000 bail. Being the money hungry person he was, Love decided to bond him out, only on the promise that he would work for him when he got out. Love put any animosity he had towards Mark and put him down with him. Mark would work his phone at night, while Love took the daytime shift. Lani loved this idea because Love would come in the house early, but Marie was the one suffering.

Lani didn't like the idea though of the two of them doing business together. She got a bad vibe from Mark, especially since she knew he was beating on her friend. Lani couldn't stand a man who beat on females. She felt any guy who would beat on a female, was a punk who deserved to get their ass whopped by a real nigga. He may not have fucked up any money, but Lani knew what she was talking about because not soon after that, they weren't hanging anymore and Love had it out for him.

When Love saw one of his fiends one day and the fiend told him Mark told him not to call Love's phone anymore to call his phone instead, Love immediately knew he was a snake in the grass. When he asked Mark about it, Mark denied it. Love remembered fiends telling him his shit wasn't as powerful as it used to be and he automatically knew Mark was "double juggling." He was serving the customers Love's work and also his own. Since Love looked at himself as being "real," he didn't want to surround himself with anyone else who wasn't on his level, so he cut ties with him altogether. The two females stood by their men and that caused conflict between them again. Marie believed her man wasn't wrong and Lani believed her man was right. They both agreed that they should have never done business together. After that, Love wanted his $2000 back and he was going to get it even if he had to go back to his old ways.

When Donell came home, Lani did not want to see him, but he came looking for her. He knew she changed since he left. She was not the same female she was when he went to jail; she had her own

142

car and apartment, therefore he wanted her back. He wanted to act on everything he said in jail. She eventually submitted to him and she chilled with him a couple times. Every time they chilled, Donell tried to get some of that ass. Lani loved when men chased her, even if she wasn't interested. She just loved the feeling that she was wanted so highly. She was very resistant but if she wasn't with Love, she would have done Donell again. She kissed him often, which was something he never did to her because he didn't like kissing but he wanted to show her he was a changed man.

Lani would tell Marie about her dilemma and Marie could relate because she had fallen for two niggas before, so she tried to tell Lani to do what she felt was right. The crazy thing was that she got her ass beat by Mark because she didn't tell her brother that Lani was fucking with Donell again. If he and Love were still speaking, he would have probably told him his damn self.

Since they met frequently, they came close to having sex – very close. As they chilled in Lani's car in a private parking lot one night, Donell played with her, seduced and touched all over her. She gave in and hopped on his dick. She was so horney but he didn't put the dick in. The tip just touched around her pussy and before he could put it in, she stopped and got off him. She knew she shouldn't have been doing what she was doing. She had a good man, one that any female would have loved to have, and here she was about to mess it up for somebody who dissed her. She also didn't do it because he wasn't trying to put a condom on and she didn't want to mix the two. Not only that, she didn't know what hoodrat he fucked since the last time they had sex. After that incident, she fell back on him because she didn't want to lose Love and she didn't want anyone trying to make him feel like a sucker by saying *that nigga think he got shit on lock but I just fucked his girl on such and such*

143

night; because believe me, when you are in a happy relationship, nobody wants to see that so they will do anything to mess that up.

A couple days later, Love approached Donell in the park. He asked him what was going on between him and Lani; he wanted to know why he was writing his house, disrespecting him. Luckily Love didn't know anything new that happened between them; he only wanted to know why he was writing Lani. Donell told him they were cool and he didn't mean to disrespect him, he was only going by what Lani told him. After that, Lani really left Donell alone, that was too close.

After they stayed in their apartment for about a year, Lani and Love decided to move. They moved out of New Haven to Milford, which was about ten minutes away. They thought they would be safer in Milford since it was mainly a "white" city. They moved into luxury condos. Their condo came equipped with a washer and dryer in the apartment, a swimming pool, 24 hour gym, basketball court, and other amenities. They paid a thousand dollars a month for rent; she was twenty-one and they were living it up – their own way.

Love would always tell her he would get her a ring. She liked hearing that but she thought he was joking, so she never paid attention to it. Him saying that only made her realize just how much he really loved her. He even put the ring on layaway. She knew this because Marie told her everything.

Lani got Love a cell phone in her name, so she had the password to his voicemail. She never suspected Love was cheating, but she never put it past him either, after all, he was a man. He was perhaps the only man she was more lenient on with trust. But she became suspicious after she heard a female on his voicemail. She was lying next to him when he checked his voicemail and since cell phones are so loud, she heard a female's voice. Love turned the volume down and ended the call because Lani was next to him. She noticed that and went in the other room and checked the voicemail. The female on the other end said she was returning his call and to call her back. She was hurt and she approached Love about it. He claimed the girl was a friend of his boy in jail and she was calling for him. She did not want to believe that but she did and she didn't let Love know it. After that, he did not want a phone in her name anymore – most likely out of guilt and so he could do his thing discreetly. That same day, he got the ring off layaway and left it at Marie's house.

Two weeks later, he proposed. He took her out to eat and while they were out he gave Marie the keys to their apartment. She put rose pedals on the floor, ran a bath water with roses, put candles everywhere, put a cake on the bedroom dresser, lingerie and the ring next to the cake. When they arrived home, Lani was surprised. When she saw the cake which read "Will you marry me," and the two and a half carat princess cut ring next to it, she burst out crying. He didn't even get on his knees, he just asked, "Will You?"

Lani was getting married. She was twenty-one with a big ass rock on her finger. She never imagined that; that was the last of her thoughts. She definitely made females jealous and with the jealousy came the hate. She fell in love even more with Love because she was now clear as to exactly how he felt, as if it wasn't evident before. That made her happy she didn't cheat on him.

After word got out Lani was engaged, a flock of niggas tried to talk to her. I guess it's true when they say "you're always wanted when someone else has you." She had grown up and she was not the street-roaming, crack-selling, fitted-wearing, weed-smoking tomboy they once knew. Every dude was trying to holla at her, from old ones to new ones. Mauri tried to holla as if he had a chance,

145

niggas from around her way tried to holla and of course Donell continued his quest. When he heard she was engaged, he was pissed and thought any chance he had in the past was out the window; that still didn't stop him from trying though.

Chapter Eleven: Drama

Marie was still having her problems with Candy and it got worse. Candy vowed she would fuck Torey when he got home and she even wrote him while he was incarcerated. Ironically, when Torey came home, Mark was in jail. He had been arrested again because his second so-called baby's mother called the cops on him and he was already on the run for a failure to appear. And once again, Marie was pregnant. Lani tried to persuade her to keep it, and she really thought she was going to keep it. After a few weeks though, she decided she did not want a baby while he was in jail because she would be miserable. She decided to abort it once again.

Since Lani and Marie shared a rental because they were in an accident in Marie's car and Lani sold her car, Marie came to pick Lani up from work. When she saw who was in the car, she was pissed. It was Torey. He had just come home and she was even more pissed when they brought Lani home to her house. Lani tried to play it off and ask them why they were bringing her to her aunt's house to throw Torey off because she did not trust him one bit.

Marie still loved Torey, she had his name tattooed on her and he had hers done in jail. Torey probably loved Marie more on a level that she would do anything for him because he was a lame nigga who depended on females to support him. He was the type who would be jealous of a female who had more money than him, which were most females because he was broke. He didn't know how to hustle on his own, so he was a neighborhood stick-up kid; but he was more of a sucker than anything. Guns were what made him tough but it's only so long fake thugs can pretend. There were times when Lani and Marie watched him get slapped and he didn't do anything but go get his gun. He was more than a sucker.

When he came home, he went looking for Marie at her job. While he was in jail, he told her he would get her back from Mark. He even said he would rob Mark; they had prior disagreements so that would be nothing for him to act on. Marie was always weak for him no matter how lame he was so she was back with him openly, but kept it hidden from Mark as if the streets wouldn't talk.

For as long as she knew him, Lani never trusted Torey. He was too sneaky and he was a jealous ass nigga. He wasn't the Mark type of jealous, but rather the "no having money, I'm envious of the next motherfucker," type of jealous. When he was in jail, he would ask about Love and who he was. He only heard of him because niggas in jail said Love was a real nigga getting that money. And one thing about the jails, they make it seem like more than what it really is; probably because they're not there so they really don't know shit. Torey would say he wanted Love to put him on when he got out. Lani didn't want Love anywhere near him because she knew what kind of person he was. When he got out, he was persistent in meeting Love.

Torey became friends with Candy when he got out. From the very beginning, Love would say he had a motive. Lani believed that too. She knew Candy's motive was to break Marie and Mark up by exposing her dealings with Torey. Torey was most likely assisting her in that mission. Why wouldn't they, they would both get what they wanted.

148

One night while Lani and Love were having a nice evening out at the movies, Lani received a call from Marie. "Lani, why I'm over here picking Torey up and Candy is out here with these chicks trying to show off." Marie explained.

"Are you serious, are you okay?" Lani asked.

"Yeah, I'm straight but she got me blocked in."

"Oh, you can't leave."

"No, she got me blocked in and she outside my car talking madd shit." While Marie was talking to Lani, Love heard everything. He grabbed Lani and left the movie theater to go check on his sister. As they were leaving, Torey got on the phone with Lani and tried to tell her Marie was okay. When Love heard his voice, he snatched the phone.

"Yo B, I don't know you like that but I don't like how you treating my sister. I'm coming to make sure she straight and when I see you I'm gonna slap you. So you better go get your guns or whatever else." Lani did not want him to say that. She knew Torey was a punk and he really would get a gun. She also knew fear was a person's worst enemy and Torey would shoot out of fear. On the way there, Lani tried to persuade Love not to go, saying it wasn't worth it and to leave it alone, but he didn't listen. He said he only wanted to talk to Torey, but that wasn't what he had Torey thinking. Lani knew there was disaster waiting ahead.

When they arrived, there was a crowd waiting. Candy was no longer there and Torey was waiting outside the car. When Love got out the car, Marie ran over to Lani who was sitting in the passenger side. "Lani, why are you doing this, why are you letting this happen?" Marie said crying.

"What, what are you talking about? He got a gun?"

149

"Yes, I don't want nothing to happen to my brother." Everyone was blaming Lani for bringing him over there. One of Nisha's cousins, Tee, even asked Lani what was wrong with her.

"That is your fiancée, what is wrong with you bringing him over here?" Tee asked.

"First of all, I told him not to come over here do it look like I'm driving?" Lani defended herself. As Love approached Torey to talk, Torey tried to act hard. He flashed the gun at Love to let him know he had a gun on him. While they were arguing, Marie got between them and said,

"Torey, please don't do nothing to my brother." That angered Love. She boosted Torey's ego and made him seem like something he wasn't. Love did not fear him, whether he had a gun or not because he knew if Torey had put the gun down, that would have been it for him. Love grabbed his sister and told her to get in the car. While he was pushing her to the car, Torey was walking over to Lani with a mean face.

"Why you bring him over here? You want him to get hurt?" Torey asked Lani. Lani thought he was going to shoot her. *No this bitch ass nigga not trying to act hard like I don't know him. He need to put that gun down so my man can beat his ass,* Lani thought. She knew he was a pussy and she didn't like how he was trying to play her future husband. She wanted him to put the gun down so bad because she knew Love would beat that ass. After it seemed to get a little worse, Lani decided to call the cops. She wasn't the type to snitch on a nigga, but if Torey would have shot her man who she loved so much, she would have made sure his ass paid.

When Tee heard Lani on the phone with the cops, she quickly blurted out to Torey, "Chill, leave yo, Lani calling the cops." After a few more minutes of arguing, Love finally said "no beef." He was

150

done trying to talk and Torey wanted to show off. He got in the car and pulled off before the cops could arrive.

Love was heated. He had been insulted by a pussy ass nigga. He dealt with much tougher dudes than Torey and he wasn't going to let him get away with that. He also told Lani to never call the cops no matter what was going on. He didn't care if he was lying in the middle of the street with a bullet in his head, he didn't want the cops involved in nothing. Right after that, Lani received a call from Marie. "You didn't tell the cops his name right?" She asked, with Torey sitting in the passenger side of the car.

When Love got home, he dressed in all black and was headed out the door. Lani was scared, she cried her heart out to him not to go but he promised her nothing would happen to him and he kissed her. He said he would borrow his cousin's Oozi and give Torey the discipline he needed to let him know who he was. Lani didn't want him to be in jail for murder, but Love was concerned about his pride. She just sat crying.

About twenty minutes later, Love returned. "I couldn't do it baby. All I was thinking about was you. Plus, Miz wouldn't let me do it either. He told me not to do it like that. Fuck it, that dude is going to get what he deserve." Torey didn't even know he could have died that night.

Marie continued to deal with Torey even after what he did to her brother. Since Tracey didn't like Lani it was the perfect time to get at her. She said since Love said he would slap Torey, she was going to slap Marie and Lani. Lani did not like that at all, and she was even more upset that Marie was still going over Tracey's house. Tracey was still being phoney to her and Marie was feeding into it.

Torey got what he was going to get a lot sooner than Love thought. Torey was shot in both legs the very next night. Every one thought Love did it, but Love was in New York at the time getting more drugs. As much as Lani would have liked, luckily Torey didn't die or Love may have been indicted. Torey knew his assailant so he knew Love didn't do it. He was shot by someone he robbed in the past – what goes around comes around. Love wasn't the only dude Torey had to worry about. There were plenty more dudes with prices on his head. After he was shot, he claimed he didn't care about Love anymore and he wanted to squash the beef so he didn't have to be looking over his shoulder. Love wasn't trying to hear that though because he wanted his revenge.

Marie was still with Torey. She was by his bedside everyday when he got shot, even though another girl he was messing with was there too. The girl, Klarrissa, was a girl everyone knew from high school. It was ironic because just a couple months prior, Marie was beefing with her because she heard she was messing with Mark. Marie heard Torey was messing with her and also heard Tracey put him on with her while he was in jail. He must have been shocked when he saw how she looked because she was definitely raised by gorillas. Torey claimed he only used her for visits, but when he got home he was fucking her and he didn't care about what Marie thought. He would even tell Marie about their sex life. He claimed he was only with her because she brought him sneakers and when she sucked him off, she put skittles and mints in her mouth. Even knowing this, Marie still didn't leave him alone.

Lani told her mother about the incident that happened with Love and Torey. At this time, Lee loved Love like a son because she saw how happy he made her daughter. Not only that, she liked him as a person because she could talk to him and see he had a good head on his shoulder. When Lani told her mother about Tracey saying she would slap her when she saw her, Lee went sick.

152

Unbeknownst to Lani, Lee told Lani's cousins, who were some wild grimlin' type of chicks about what Tracey said. They got down for the cause and didn't have any problem approaching a bitch. Lani's cousin Teda didn't like Tracey to begin with and promised she would see her about what she said. When her cousin Teda and her other cousin Keyshia (the one she and her mother were living with) saw Tracey in the Taurus, they approached her on the situation.

Teda and Keyshia were at the bar getting a drink. They were already drunk and when Teda noticed Tracey, it was on. Keyshia had her back to Tracey who was right next to her. Since Keyshia didn't know how she looked, Teda pointed her out to Keyshia. Teda was whispering to Keyshia telling her Tracey was behind her and Keyshia turned around to Tracey, pointed her way and said, "This her? This Tracey?" Teda nodded her head in confirmation and Keyshia continued, "What is your problem with Lani?" Tracey looked at her confused and responded,

"Who? Lani Who?" As if she didn't know who Lani was.

"Love's girlfriend." Keyshia responded.

"No, Love's fiancée." Teda corrected.

"You said you was gonna slap her, cuz if you gon' slap her then I will slap you right now." Keyshia added.

"No, I don't have a problem with Lani. Her and Marie were just at my house the other day." She was lying her ass off so she wouldn't get that ass beat. She knew these chicks were about their business and she did not want to get her ass whopped in the Jump.

"Oh, okay, just making sure." Keyshia responded, not knowing she was lying. When Keyshia and Teda told Lani what happened the next day, Lani was hysterical. She told them that Tracey was lying and they told her if they would have known that, they would have whopped her ass right there. Lani was happy they did that, and from then on, Tracey didn't have anything to say except behind her back.

Marie's constant dealings with Torey made Love disown his sister saying she was "disloyal." He hated her for what she did and would never get over it. Although everyone in her family hated Torey, and now hated him even more, that still didn't stop Marie from seeing him.

One night after Torey got shot, Marie brought him to her aunt's restaurant to talk with her mom. Since he used a walker to walk, she was helping him out the car. Love happened to ride by and saw this. Torey was now in his hood – by himself. He was also hurt that his sister was catering to him despite the bad blood between them. Love initially decided to get a gun, but he felt that was too hot, especially with the police substation a few feet down the street. Instead, he went to get a bat. Just as he arrived back to the restaurant, Marie was pulling the car to the back of the restaurant so Torey wouldn't have to go down the hump in the front. When Marie saw her brother, she walked to his window. When she saw the look in his eye, she got scared because she knew something was about to happen. His eyes were bloodshot red. She tried to talk to him but he gave one word responses. She thought he would pull off but as she walked away from the car, Love ran past her and encountered Torey. "Oh so you want to pull guns out on niggas, huh?" Love said hiding the bat behind his back.

"Man, fuck you." Torey said. When Love pulled the bat from behind him, Torey's eyes became fully dilated and he screamed like a bitch. He used his walker as a force field and tried to run back inside the restaurant, but Love knocked it away and he fell to the ground. Love began beating his wounded legs but he was unable to do the damage he wanted to because they were stuck in the doorway which was a tight space. Torey cried out, "Marie, Marie, get your brother, get your brother." After a while, Marie got between them and Love hit her too and ran off.

All of Torey's friends and family thought either Lani set him up or Marie. Tracey cut dealings with Marie after that and her family wanted to sue Sandra's because of what happened. His mother thought Love started trouble with Torey for nothing, but after she found out the reasons behind what was going on, she quickly changed her mind. She told her son he got what he deserved and he was lucky he didn't get shot again. She then wiped her hands with the situation and prayed for the best. After Marie cleared herself, he tried to ask her where her brother lived. Although she and Love weren't on good terms and she loved Torey so much, she didn't put Love and Lani in danger by telling him.

After that incident, the beef died down. Torey felt everything was even and he didn't want any more problems with Love. Love also felt they were even. Torey was more concerned with the dude who shot him. Love wasn't going for that though because although Torey wasn't a threat to him, he still kept one eye open.

Also following that incident, a bunch of other shit began to happen. All of a sudden, after never hearing anything, Lani heard Love cheated on her. Marie called her one day and told her what she was told.

"Lani, I have to tell you something but you have to promise me you are not going to say anything. Let me handle it." Marie said.

"Alright, fine." Lani said, not knowing what she was about to hear concerned her man.

"Well I was with Tee today and you know how I have the picture of you and my brother up on the dashboard?"

"Yeah."

155

"Well she was looking at it and she was like, 'this your brother?' So I was like yeah and she was like 'he fuck with my cousin.' So I was like your cousin who? She said her name is Pam. So I was like no he don't, she is wifey, she got a big ass ring on her finger. I wasn't going to tell you and I talked to my brother earlier but he just wasn't trying to hear it and he said it wasn't true so I was just going to let it go but I felt I had to tell you." After hearing that, Lani's stomach sunk to her feet. She was hurt from hearing that and she couldn't understand how Marie was telling her not to mention that to her man; knowing if she heard that about her man, she would disregard the promise of not saying anything.

"Oh, word, she said that, huh." Lani said nervously with a crack in her voice as if she was holding back her tears. "Niggas ain't shit man I swear."

"Tell me about it yo. You know if we had millions we wouldn't care about no nigga right?"

"Why you say that?"

"Cuz yo, you would? I wouldn't cuz if I had madd money, I wouldn't fall in love with nobody. All I would need a nigga for his the pipe and even still, I could probably buy one that felt exactly like it. At any given time I could hop on a flight and go cross country or something and forget about the nigga. I would treat the niggas just how they treat us."

"Yeah you right, but that's beside the point. We don't have millions. I'm trying to see what's good with what you just said."

"Yeah, but it's straight. Pam is P's sister. I don't know if you saw her before, but she is P's sister." Lani remembered she had P's direct connect number in her phone and she decided to call him to get Pam's number because she wanted to talk to her and see what was really good. She hung up with Marie and told her she would not

156

mention anything to Love, instead, she called Pam to get to the bottom of the allegations.

The girl already knew Lani was calling because P called her to see if it was okay to give Lani her number, so she already knew what to expect. The female told Lani she was messing with Love about two years prior. Lani was with him then, so she listened. She told Lani he would come to her house at night and leave in the morning. She said it was nothing serious, they were just fucking. She told Lani to call her if he tried to deny it. She was nice about the situation and Lani respected that.

When Love got in, Lani went sick on him. He admitted to knowing the girl and said she was a chickenhead that he used to sleep with before he went to jail (he didn't know Lani then). When Lani got Pam on the phone, they both stuck with their stories. Love was calling the girl a chickenhead and he also told Lani "fuck her" for believing what people say. Lani believed Pam and Love didn't like that. He begged her to believe him. Lani didn't break up with him, but she didn't like what she heard and she kept her eyes open from then on.

After hearing the accuser was the friend of Tracey, Lani began to analyze what she was told. Two years prior, Love stayed with his grandmother and Lani stayed the night with him every night. If she wasn't at his house, he was at hers, so how could he be with the girl. It was nothing like the situation with her and Kane; Love was with her every night. Lani came to the conclusion that Tracey probably told her to say those things. They say never listen to people when you're in a relationship because when you have something good, everyone will try to end it. Although some things are lies, some are true, and if they are not 100% true, they have

157

some truth in it. It's up to you to do without the he say, she say altogether. Sometimes seeing it provides the best truth.

Lani would continue to hear about shit the girl would say. She would threaten to slap Lani, as if Tracey's threat didn't send the message. Lani didn't know what their beef was because they didn't have a disagreement on the phone. If there was a disagreement, she should have let it be known right then and there instead of saying shit behind Lani's back. She would also say Love brought her sneakers often and gave her money. Lani didn't even confront Love when she would hear that because for one, the girl looked stupid. Love was not that generous. If it was true, why would she brag about getting something she could buy herself? She bragged about some $65 LeBron James sneakers; hell if she was gonna brag about some sneakers, it should have at least been some Jordans. Why settle for less when the nigga had it. Lani was getting more than sneakers. She got a thousand dollar rent paid, a thousand dollars cash here and there, sneakers, outfits, cars, he even paid her a couple hundred dollars to help him bag up. Not to mention the big two and a half carat rock she had. So she really didn't care about some seventy dollar pair of sneakers, she shouldn't have settled for something she could buy herself. Lani just sat back and laughed at the fans she had who made her feel like a star.

After that incident though, Lani became suspicious of Love's activities. Every little thing she thought he was cheating on her. When she called Love's cousin one day to try to plan him a surprise birthday party at Jay-Z's 40-40 club, she heard Love in the background talking. She told his cousin not to tell her she was on the phone because it was a surprise, so Love didn't know who was on the phone. As Lani was talking to D, the conversation Love was having in the background sounded fishy. It sounded like a conversation he was having with a female. As analytical as Lani was or any chick for that matter, she could tell if a man was talking to a homeboy or a female. As she began to talk lower and slower in order to hear what Love was saying in the background, his conversation came to a cease as if he got out the car or hung up. Immediately Lani became suspicious and thought D tapped Love and told him Lani was on the phone to cover his boy. Lani left it alone because she didn't know what was going on, and that was that.

Love and Marie still weren't speaking. Marie was hurt. She missed her brother. Lani would throw things in his ear here and there to get them back speaking, but that wasn't enough for him to forgive her. He promised he wouldn't deal with his sister ever again. He stated, "she went against the grain. She's still my sister but I just won't deal with her. I will only love her from a distance. Hopefully she'll get her mind right and leave those bum dudes alone." And that was the way it was going to be – at least for the time being.

Chapter Twelve: Broken Hearted

After things died down, Lani felt more at ease. At home though, was a different story; she and Love had their own problems. Lani would often start arguments with him because he would come in the house late. She made the mistake of accepting it early on in the game, so now he was used to it. She eventually got fed up and they argued more and more about it. Lani had mentioned him cheating before, but he would tell her he didn't have time to cheat because he was out there getting money. Although those were the same lines Donell would tell her, she believed him because seeing is believing and she saw him making the money. As a matter of fact, she applied for a gun permit to protect herself. Since she was Love's girl and everyone thought of him as some big time dude, anyone was prone to attack her.

Lani never thought Love would cheat on her. That was the last thing in the back of her mind but they say one's solemate can feel deceit. That statement is absolutely true. Since she and love stopped celebrating holidays like Christmas and Valentine's Day because everyday was a holiday in their relationship, Lani decided to work on Valentine's Day. She worked the whole day and wanted to talk to her baby. While at work, she called and called him but he didn't have his phone on. When she finally got through to him, he told her he took his cousin to the jail to visit her baby's father. She just knew he was with someone else, but that was just how she felt at the time. She knew deep down inside he was doing something he

160

wasn't supposed to be doing but she had no proof. He may not have gotten caught then if he was doing something, but ten days later, he did.

While Lani was on her way home in the midst of a blizzard one wintery evening, she called her man to see when he would be coming home. Instead of Love answering, his cousin Twenty answered his phone. Lani didn't like Twenty too much because she knew what he was about. Though it wasn't right, she didn't like him because he was a player; as a person, he was cool though. He put his girlfriend through a bunch of shit she didn't deserve and Lani didn't want Love around that. Twenty told Lani Love was in the store getting something to eat. Lani called back ten minutes later and talked to Love briefly before his phone hung up. Love had two phones so she called them both and they both went straight to voicemail. Lani had stomach butterflies and knew something was up.

She waited around, but didn't hear anything from Love. She called him over and over but got the voicemail. She was livid. Being the obsessive person she had become, she played around with numbers one night prior to this night and cracked the password to one of his phones. Around 2 a.m., she checked his voicemail and heard a woman's voice. The female just said hello and hung up. Lani heard females on this same phones' voicemail before but never mentioned it to him. The females never said anything worth him changing the password so she never said anything. She wanted to wait until she had solid proof he was cheating to mention anything.

After a while, Lani's emotions became mixed with paranoia, anxiety and rage. She didn't know if something happened to her man or what. What she did know however, was as soon as his ass walked in that door, all paranoia and worriness would be out the door; he would get his ass flipped on. Love arrived in the house at 3 a.m., five hours after Lani talked to him.

"Where you been?" Lani asked.

"What?" That's something all men do. A woman asks a question; they heard the question, but they answer with a question to get time to think of an answer to the original question.

"You heard me, where you been?"

"Oh...I was at the bar with my boys. Why?"

"What time did you leave? And your boys who?"

"I was with JK and them. We left like 1:30." Love didn't mention Twenty's name. He knew exactly what he was doing. He knew what Lani was capable of and since she didn't know his other friends (or their phone numbers), she couldn't call them to catch Love out, but she could call Twenty. He lied to her anyway. It was Thursday night, clubs and bars closed at 12:45 so how did he leave at 1:30?

"One thirty huh, when clubs end at 12:45?"

"Lani, I don't know what time we left."

"Yeah, whatever." Lani knew he was lying and she was determined to get to the bottom of it. Love went to sleep immediately; he was drunk. When he went to sleep, Lani went in his drawer and got his car key. He kept his phone in the car and that's what she went to get. She stayed in the living room and searched through his phone. She noticed a number at eight o'clock which was also on his phone at two a.m. in the received call log. Lani wasn't even able to get through to him at that time. She wanted to know who was more important that he didn't answer or call her, so she called the number back.

A female answered and Lani paused for a few. Her heart dropped as she hoped it was the girlfriend of JK or another friend.

After the second hello, Lani spoke. "Hello, somebody called an 809 number?" Lani asked playing reverse psychology on the girl.

"No." The girl responded. *Fuck it this bitch gon' act stupid, let me just get straight to the point,* Lani thought.

"You know Love?" Lani asked before the girl could hang up.

"Yeah." The girl said in a smart tone. Lani was quiet. "Yeah." The girl said again.

"You fuck with him?"

"Ask him." The girl said and hung up. *Ask him huh, this bitch wanna act stupid over the phone. That's exactly why chicks call phones back and be actin' all crazy cuz the moment one call on some calm shit, they wanna act like fools,* Lani thought. Lani called back. "Hello." The girl said in an aggravated, it's four in the morning tone.

"What you mean ask him, I'm asking you. That's my fiancée so I'm trying to see what's good. I ain't marrying no nigga if he tryin' to play…"

Before Lani could finish her sentence, the girl blurted out, "Well you see he wasn't home tonight, you do the math," and hung up again. Lani got off the couch and stormed into the bedroom with anger and rage once again.

"DaRon, DaRon, get your ass up right now." Lani said angrily with the phone in her hand. She was heated this chick tried to make her seem like some flow like she didn't have Love on lock.

"What Lani, what."

"Whose number is 7-7-3-1-8-6-4?"

"What?"

"You heard me nigga, 7-7-3-1-8-6-4."

"I don't know." He said half asleep.

"Well there's some chick saying you was with her tonight."

163

"What?" Love said.

"Call this chick back cuz she said she was with you tonight." Love was fully awake now. When he registered what Lani was saying and saw the phone in her hand, he slapped the shit out her. Before then, he never slapped her or put his hands on her before except in a playful manner. Lani tried to fight him back but he just grabbed her hands and held her so she couldn't hit him. She didn't care about the slap, no, that was the least of her worries; she was more concerned with him cheating, the slap could wait. "You gon' slap me cause you got caught." Lani shot his phone and broke it on the wall. He picked it up and tried to put it back together. "Call this chick."

Love did everything but call the girl. It took him ten minutes for him to say, "Call her." Lani called her back and put the call on speaker phone.

"Hello." The voice on the other end said.

"Hello." Love said. "Somebody called Love?"

"Yeah, Londa called you Love." The girl said as a matter of factly.

"Who is Londa?" Love asked.

"Who is Londa. You know who Londa is. You was just with us." The girl on the phone wasn't the same girl Lani talked to.

"I was just with ya'll? No I wasn't."

"Yes you was, you bugging Love."

"Well who is this?"

"This is Star."

"Who is Star? Well somebody just told my girl I was with them."

"Yeah, you was, and why is your girl calling here?" After that, Lani just hung up.

164

"You a fucking liar. You ain't shit." Love stood and prepared to get dressed. He finally decided to come clean.

"Yeah I know them, but I don't fuck with any of them. I was with them tonight, but I was only there because of my nigga."

"Your nigga who? Twenty?"

"Yeah. We just rode around with them. That's it." Lani didn't believe his whole story. She knew more was going on. She just burst out crying. She had never been hurt by anyone like that before because she never loved anyone as much as she did Love. She ran into the living room and cried hysterically like someone died. Love followed her and she just couldn't believe him.

"How could you do this to me?" Love got dressed and left. He couldn't say anything to Lani to make it better. Lani called Marie and they talked until seven in the morning.

The next day, Lani couldn't even concentrate at work. She was able to take the night off because she was crying and couldn't function. She went home to rest and put her thoughts on the table. While she was there, Love came and started packing a bag. He told her he was going to Atlanta (where his uncle lived) for a couple days. *No this nigga not leavin', I'm supposed to be leaving. He did wrong.* Typical guy, always running from the situation or making the woman seem like the bad one.

Lani tried not to think about the situation, but she couldn't help it. She didn't have any proof that he cheated, but she felt it. She couldn't really trust the female because she could have been saying anything. She started asking people about the females and who they were. A guy Marie worked with knew the chicks and told Marie the girls were "fly." *Yeah they fly alright*, Lani imagined. Lani hearing that only made her want to know who the girls were even more. She wanted to know what she had to compete with as if she had to to begin with.

Before Love left for Atlanta, he apologized to Lani and told her he needed to get away to think because he messed up and he didn't want to lose her. He never admitted fucking the girl, he only said he shouldn't have been riding around with them. That made Lani feel better, but she didn't want him to go. He promised he would call her once he got there.

By eleven o'clock, he hadn't called and Lani wanted to talk to him so she attempted to get his uncle's cell phone number. After numerous calls to his family members, she received a number to one of his cousin's house. Vanessa was one of his girl cousins who moved from Connecticut to Alabama. She told anybody how it was regardless of how they felt. When Lani called her and asked her for Love's uncle number, she went off.

"Girl, you know you shouldn't be calling him. He messed up, not you. He gone now so I would not be thinking about him. I would be partying and I would turn my phone off, make him wonder what I'm doin. You get that nigga girl. If he giving you a thousand dollars, you make him give you fifteen hundred. Show him who's boss. He messed up, not you. Shit my man know. Let his ass pull some shit like that on me, his clothes would be right outside. If I was you, I would not talk to him the whole time he down there. I would move my clothes out the house and when he came home to an empty house, his ass would know. You got you a cute little boyfriend and he getting a little money, so girls are gonna try to holla. They don't care if he got a girl or not, you know how it is. You just have to stand your ground and let that nigga know what he got. You young and he older so he think he can run over you a little, so you have to be on your game even more. I'm gonna give you the number, call if you want to but I'd teach his ass a lesson. You need to teach him a lesson so he know not to do no bullshit again."

Vanessa was absolutely right in every way, but Lani called anyway. She just didn't have the strength to do it. Besides, she didn't want to listen to Vanessa and the plan backfire on her and she be the one assed out in the end. Aside from that, Lani was young and Love was an older man, so she hadn't acquired that womanly wisdom yet.

Lani was miserable the whole time he was gone. She had never slept without him in two and a half years and now that she had to, she couldn't sleep. The house felt so empty without him. There was no one to cook breakfast for, he wasn't there to kiss her before he left and tell her he loved her, there was no one to hold her, and it just wasn't the same. Aside from that, she was scared to sleep in the house by herself because Love was always there to protect her; and for some strange reason, now that he was gone, she heard every single noice in the house.

Lloyd Banks of G-Unit came to perform at a small club in New Haven and she went to the performance. The venue was live and it seemed as if the whole New Haven was in the building. From the outside, one would have thought Lani was enjoying herself, but inside, she was an emotional wreck. While there, she called Love constantly. Lloyd Banks was two hours late so she decided to leave because she wanted to talk to Love. As she was leaving, Banks was coming in but she still went out. She loved her man and besides, it wasn't like she could leave with Banks.

Lani talked with Love everyday while he was in the A-town. He told her he was getting his mind right and analyzing his life. He told her when he got back he would get focused and do what he had to do so he could get out the game. He also told her he would watch

167

who he surrounded himself with so he wouldn't get caught up in anymore bullshit. Lani truly believed what he was saying and knew things would be different.

When Love came back home, Lani picked him up from the airport. When she saw him, she hugged him tight and he hugged her tightly too; they missed each other. When they got home, they made love like it was the last time. While they were having sex, Lani made it very clear that she wasn't letting no female take him away from her. She made an investment in Love and she wasn't about to let him go that easily. He vowed he would make a change and would treat her like he used to.

Things were going good for about a week. Love showed more affection than ever before. But after Lani felt a bump on his testicle, things began to get very strange. Love had a dream that woke him out his sleep one night. He woke up and grabbed Lani tightly. He kissed her and told her he loved her. He told her he had a dream she left him. The next day he told her he was jerking off and after he came he went to the bathroom and it was burning while he was peeing. Lani told him that was normal because there were times after they had sex that she would use the bathroom and she would experience slight burning that lasted for a second; which was normal due to the irritation from a man's sperm so she didn't think anything of it. Then he told her there was pus coming out his dick, and he showed her the dry pus on his pajamas. She told him to go to the doctors. She still didn't think anything of it. He told her the doctors told him he had a bladder infection.

Love began to act even stranger. He brought her flowers home one night and he pushed the issue of her having health insurance; he eventually paid for the insurance. While hanging his coat up in the closet one day, Lani went in Love's pocket and pulled

168

out a prescription. Love had been prescribed doxycycline which Lani knew were for infections because they prescribed her that after her abortions and surgery; she figured that was for his bladder infection.

Lani still didn't think anything of it until one night, Lani and Marie were about to go out to a bar. Lani decided to ride down Liberty Street, which was a street he hustled on and also the street she heard the girl he cheated with lived on. She found his car on the corner parked and thought he was at the girl's house. She parked behind his car and called him. He answered so she knew he couldn't have been with a girl. He lied to her and told her he was in another town though. After a brief argument, he came outside to her car. They continued to argue and even broke up with each other because Love told her he was sick of her making issues out of small stuff like him lying. What men and women don't understand is that small lies eventually turn into big lies.

All of a sudden, he became sentimental on her. He had been acting real strange the days prior to this night. She hadn't had sex with him in a week and he was being exceptionally nice. She knew he said he would be a better man, the man she knew when he came home from jail, but he was acting weird. She asked him what was going on and he told her to take him home and they would talk about it.

She was nervous on the way home. He began saying he would never hurt her intentionally and she was where his heart was. She had stomach butterflies and she didn't know what was going on.

When they got home, Love grabbed her and laid her on top of him. He told her he loved her and she told him the same. While they were in a conversational mood, she had to ask him one question she wanted to know since the incident with the girl.

169

"Baby, I just want to know one thing. It's been killing me since it happened. I won't get mad. I just have to know to bring closure to my life. Did you fuck her?" Love began shedding tears as he sat up. Lani knew good news wasn't about to come. After a brief pause, Love responded.

"I fucked her...but there's more."

"Oh god, what happened?" Love was silent. "Did you get somebody pregnant cause that's the worst thing you could do to me."

"No, I didn't get anyone pregnant."

"So what happened?"

"Okay...so I fucked the girl. I felt guilty that's why I went to Atlanta. I got my head clear, my uncle schooled me and told me to do the right thing if I didn't want to lose my girl. I come back home, everything is good between us, next thing I know, my dick is burning, I got pus coming out my shit. I go to the doctor, I fuck around and got BURNT." Lani was totally speechless. After brief silence, she responded calmer than she should have been. "You what? You got BURNT. So you fucked that bitch raw?"

"No. I used a condom. It popped and I stopped. It was a one night stand."

"So you didn't even know this girl?"

"No, I went over there cuz it was Twenty's show. I was drunk and the chick Londa was all over me." Lani couldn't believe what she was hearing. She had never been burnt before and she got burnt by the man she thought was her solemate. She expected to get burnt by anyone else other than him. The way Donell was out there with whomever he was out there with, she thought she would get burnt by him if anything. She put her coat on and headed out the door. He begged her not to go, saying they should work it out together, but Lani left anyway. She didn't know what to do. She didn't know

170

whether she should stay or go. This was indeed the worst feeling ever.

After analyzing what she was told, Lani understood just how real Karma was. She also knew that whatever is in the dark shall come to light eventually. Lani didn't even have to call the girl back if she wanted to find out he cheated. If she would have waited a few, it would have come out just as it did. He got what he deserved, but he involved her in his deceit. She figured if anyone knew better, it would be him. His mother and brother died of AIDS; that was more than a lesson. He went by looks. Everything that glitters isn't gold; in case America hasn't learned it already, anyone can get a disease.

As Lani sat in the parking lot of her complex, all she could think about was how much her family adored him and how they thought he was a good man. She thought about all the sweet things he said to her, all the sweet things he did, and how he changed her life. She thought about all they had been through and all the times she was there for him in his time of need. She recalled when she went up top to cop drugs for him – something no other female probably would have never done. She thought about the times they drove to New York to cop work; she knew she had played her part well. She couldn't understand why he would wait until he proposed to her to start acting up, or at least why it had to come out after that.

Overnight he made her change her mind and believe there were some good men out there and just like that he took that away. She began to question his love for her. She had the ring, but could he have proposed to shut her up. Did he think just because he was taking care of home and put a ring on her finger that he could cheat on her? She wondered why he never listened to her words. Lani would always tell him, "watch those hoes, bitches ain't shit, they will get you for your money," and like a fool, he had sex with a hoe and

171

brought something home. She got out the car and went back in the house to let him have it.

"You cheap as fuck." Lani said bursting in the door. Love just stared at her. "You a stupid ass nigga. I gave you everything, I gave you my all. I put my trust in you. It wasn't enough for you to just fuck a bitch, but you had to fuck a bitch raw. You of all people should know to strap up, you lost your family to AIDS. What if the bitch got AIDS. You got me sitting up here fucking you raw still, still sucking ya dick and you done stuck your dick in someone else raw."

"Lani, first of all, I used a rubber. It popped and I stopped. And she don't have no damn AIDS."

"How you know what she got. If you knew what she had you wouldn't have gotten burnt in the first place. How do you even know if you had a condom on, you was drunk right?"

"Yeah, but I know I put one on."

"So why you didn't know not to fuck her if you wasn't that drunk? You thought you would get away with that? I've been too good of a person to you. God made this happen. He put that fire on your ass. You know how many times I could have given up your pussy. No! You have absolutely no idea nigga. How can you say she didn't have AIDS you didn't know she even had an STD you jerk." Love just sat there silent, looking like a fool. "And how selfish of you? You knew you had something a week ago. How much longer were you going to hold out? You don't play with nobody's health. What did she give you anyway?" Lani may have felt Love should have told her right away, but in her mind, she knew if she had brought something home, she damn sure would have probably done the same thing.

172

"She gave me Chlamydia. I tried to tell you. You see I was acting strange. The dreams, the burning, the pus, I thought you would know. How can you tell someone you love that shit?"

Well shit, at least he got something he could get rid of. I can't live with no damn herpes. Lani thought. "You thought. You don't think when it comes to somebody's life? If not mines, care about yours. You don't just assume, just like you assumed the girl was clean, you made an ASS out of U and ME. And how could you do something like that to someone you love? What, were you trying to get her pregnant? Do you even care about this relationship? Did you tell the dirty bitch she burnt you?"

"For what? She probably knew she had something. I shouldn't have been dumb enough to fuck her."

"You damn right. It was a blizzard and you chose to be with someone other than your wife. That's exactly why you got what you got. You played with fire and your ass got burnt. Damn man...Why the fuck you just couldn't leave me alone? You had to pursue me. You should have just let me be and I would have been fine not knowing you. I wish I would have never met you...Damn." There was nothing he could say. Lani was hurt.

She was treated the very next day. She didn't care that her health insurance hadn't begun and she didn't care about a thousand dollar bill, she wasn't about to walk around with an STD; bad enough the time she waited was long enough to her. She had been feeling dirty since he told her, and what he told her consumed her thoughts so much, she didn't think that she could have went to the emergency room right then and there.

Now that she was treated, she had to decide what to do about Love. They still slept in the same bed, but she didn't touch him. She began to have bad dreams and on one occasion she

173

blurted out, "I Hate You" in her sleep. That really hurt Love. He knew he fucked up and lost his girl. He knew the trust was totally out the window from then on. He played all innocent like he was different and he turned out to be the same. The innocent ones are the worst kind to deal with.

Over the next few days, Lani confided in Niya, Nisha, and Marie. She needed some advice. Although she would make her own decision, she still wanted to see what they thought. Overall they told her to stay with him; which was what she wanted to do anyway, she just needed to know it was okay to stay. Because he did get burnt, she truly thought he learned his lesson and he wouldn't cheat again.

Lani even confided in her brother. She and her brother had begun to get tight and they kept in touch often. She consulted her brother about the situation to get a man's opinion. She told him everything, even about the STD. Her brother told her that he most likely didn't have a one night stand because those were played out, "especially if the girl was pretty," he told her. That crushed Lani and she didn't know what to think. That's when the insecurity began to set in. She always knew if she wasn't a dime, she knew she was an eight and her personality gave her the extra two points; but after that, she felt like a one.

Lani did something all women do when their man does something wrong; she began to feel guilty about what happened. She figured she got what she deserved. Although she never actually cheated on him, she did betray him, which may have led to him cheating. Then she thought he cheated because of the streets. He was out there hustling, getting money. He had the looks and the style, so of course there would be women coming at him. It's like being in the NBA or a celebrity and having a wife, there's women all

174

around you. You turn some down, but after a while, you just give in. Lani was making excuses for his actions. Then, she no longer hated Love; him cheating actually made her want him even more. She then turned her anger on the girl.

After Love cheated on Lani, she began to find things about herself that she thought she needed to change in order to prevent her man from looking elsewhere. Overnight, Lani decided to do away with the tomboy look, which she had already decided prior to the incident, but hadn't fully given up. Now she only wanted to wear tight jeans and shirts. She didn't really wear shoes unless she was going somewhere, but she kept tight jeans and shirts on. She made sure hair appointments weren't missed and she made sure she kept her toes done. By the grace of God, she received her gun permit two weeks after Love cheated on her because somebody would have been dead.

Lani also turned to music for support. In particular, she was feeling a slept on R & B singer named Teedra Moses. Teedra's song, "*You'll never find*," sounded like something Lani wrote. The lyrics in her song reflected exactly how she felt at the time. She hummed the words every single day, especially in the presence of Love. *Fuss fight, put you out, take you back cuz baby it's a ghetto love affair (ghetto love affair, ghetto love affairrrrrr), tell me what you know about ya man, hugging blocks, all night, when he should be home huggin' you (ohhhh ohhh), tell me what you know what a hustla' can do, for true loveeeeee. You'll never find, a better love, or a bigger foolllllll. Tell me what you know about breaking up and getting back together...Tell me what you know ya man, giving gifts **to compensate for all his shit***, Lani would often sing.

Although she forgave Love, she started pushing him away because she threw it up in his face from time to time. She began conducting investigations and gathered information on Londa and Star. She was anxious to see what the girls looked like. She found a website, intelius.com that allowed her to input the phone number she already had and was able to find what address the number belonged to and who lived in the house. After doing a background check (which cost her $50) on Londa, she was able to find her age, birthdate, last name, address, and also discovered the girl was arrested for drug possession. Lani found this strange because she noticed the girl lived in the "Jungle" at one point, which was where Love grew up and hustled. She also noticed the girl didn't live on Liberty Street which confirmed that one should never believe what they hear from someone else. She also noticed the drug charge came while she was with Love.

She began thinking about prior incidents. Love was arrested for trespassing in the "Jungle" around the same time the girl was living there. What a coincidence. Then she began to speculate that perhaps the girl worked for Love at one point and caught a drug charge behind him. She no longer thought this was a one night stand. She brought it up to Love, but he stuck with his original statement, "it was a one night stand."

Because of her pride, Lani wanted to leave him so bad, but at the same time, she loved him to death. She knew it could have been worse though. He could have been disrespecting her or he could have popped up with a kid. Hell, he could not have been coming home to her every night. He could have had chicks approaching her on some other shit, he could have had chicks answering his phone or calling her back, or he could have done worse shit which other females were going through. Instead of leaving him, she wanted to do what Vanessa told her to do in the first place and that was to make him think she was leaving.

176

As the words to Teedra Moses song, *"For a lifetime,"* echoed in the background (*You giveeeee, and you giveeeee, but you never seem to get back in returnnnn, what you giveeee, til ya heart suffers through third degree burnnnssss, and in the end, you just want to give up on loveeeeee...*), Lani just sat crying. It would take a while for her to get over what he did and she felt like she should have punished him when he did it.

After Lani talked to Love and they had the argument about the situation again because she just knew it wasn't a one night stand, she went home to pack her bags. She kept calling Love to argue with him some more and hoped he would finally come clean, but he turned his phone off. She didn't know where he was until she called his cousin D and he told her he went to New York. Lani found Love's new connect number in his drawer and called his connect. Love had left by the time she called so he didn't know she called. Lani had totally violated the code of the streets and could have gotten Love killed. Had that been back in the eighty's, they both would have been dead for sure. For all his connect knew, it could have been a set up or anything. When you're in the street, you have to stay open minded like that in order to survive. When Lani told Love she called his connect, he was ready to break up with her right then and there.

Lani was doing a bunch of things that was out of her character. She was dangerously in love and now knew exactly what Beyonce meant when she said it. She conducted a background check and she drove down the street the girl lived on a couple times; hoping someone she knew would be out there so she could hop out wearing Love's chain and hopefully be spotted by the girl. She also asked people about the girl – what type of shit was that. All because she wanted to see how the girl looked. She heard the chicks were "fly," so she damn sure wanted to see just how fly they were. They may have been fly, but one or both of them were on fire. Luckily she got her gun permit after he cheated or someone would have been dead.

When Love finally became comfortable with the situation, she was able to pick him for a description of the chicks, but that was about it. In an effort for her to leave not only them alone, but also him, he told her the chicks were bums who smoked woolies. He told her he heard they didn't live in New Haven anymore and had moved down south. She believed him and became even angrier that he fucked a basehead. She would later find out that he was lying.

While Marie was at work one day, she overheard someone call another girl "Star" and automatically assumed that was the same girl. At a club, she pointed the girl Star out to Lani. Star was with another female who fit the description Love gave her. Lani assumed it was Londa because she was short, chubby and had long hair as he described. Instead of enjoying herself in the club, she followed the girl around the whole night. She really thought it was the girl because she was in a bunch of dudes faces. After the club, they continued to follow the chicks and at one point, Lani stated loudly to Marie, "Yeah, let me call my man LOVE to see what he doing," hoping the girl would turn around and confirm she was indeed Londa. She had enough sense not to say anything to the girl because she wasn't sure if it was her; and luckily she didn't because they later found out it was not her. She was definitely out of character and acting like a young ass fifteen year old girl.

After the incident, Lani also began to go to the doctor's more frequently to make sure her health was up to par. She often went to the doctor to make sure her reproductive system was fine being that she hadn't gotten pregnant again since her ectopic pregnancy. She had a pain in her that came about after the surgery and she wanted to see what it was. After telling the doctor about her pain, he referred her to the urologist because he thought her pain could be urinary. After further investigating, Lani found out she had kidney stones and had to have kidney surgery. She began to think about the phrase that "everything happens for a reason." Had Love not burnt her, she probably would have never gone to the doctors and her kidneys would have become worse in the process.

As Lani was recovering in the house, she began to get lonely. Since it was the summertime, she thought she was missing something. She didn't stay on bed rest for the two weeks the doctor suggested and while she still had bandages on, she started hanging in the streets again. As Marie and Lani were riding up the Boston Post Road, a female named Lenoya pulled up on the side of them at the light.

Lenoya was a female Love was involved with right before he went to jail. Because he went to jail, they never got the chance to make anything happen. She went on to have a baby and lived with her baby's father. Her baby's father was actually an old boyfriend of Reasha's and a long-time friend of Lani. Marie was cool with Lenoya, but only because her baby's father and Torey were in the same jail at one time. Torey suggested she ride with Lenoya to visit him and after that they spoke to each other. Although she didn't know her, Lani didn't like her because Marie told her about a time she went in Red Coat Records to get a CD and Lenoya was in there. As soon as she entered the store, Lenoya asked her to call her brother because he tried to play her in the club. Being that Marie wanted to see how the hell he tried to play her so she could tell her friend, she called Love. She didn't really get a chance to talk to Love because as soon as he realized who it was calling from his sister's phone, all he said was "yo, what you calling me for, I got a girlfriend and I really love her"; had she called from her own phone, the conversation would have been totally different, but he didn't want Marie to go back and tell Lani anything so they never knew exactly why she called him. After that, there were a couple incidents when Marie would see her and she would ask about Love. Marie would tell Lani about it and after hearing it too many times, Lani began to think she was trying to get at Love. The last time Marie told Lani, she promised that the next time she saw her, she would approach her about it.

As Lani noticed her pull up on the side of her, she had her chance to confront her. "What's good with Kevin?" Lani asked sarcastically being that she was asking about her man.

"Oh shit, that's Lenoya?" Marie asked laughing.

"Who you?" Lenoya responded angrily.

"I'm sayin', what's up with Kevin? Pull over and we can talk." They both pulled into a gas station. As Lani opened her door, she grabbed her gun from under the seat and tucked it into her pants.

"So what's good with Kevin?" Lani asked again.

"And who you?"

"I'm sayin', Kev my nigga but when I don't see him for a long time, I don't go around asking people about him. You know who I am?"

"You look familiar."

"Well I'm Love girl and I'm trying to figure out why you asking about him." The girl then began to get loud with Lani, but as her voice elevated, Lani lifted her shirt exposing her bandage patch and gun simultaneously and said, "Yo listen, I just had surgery and shit. I ain't gon' fight you." When the girl noticed the gun, she quickly toned it down.

"Well me and my baby's father just had a fight so I thought you was a girl he was messing with. I thought I was about to have to fight again. But it ain't nothing with me and Love. I just wanted to know what was going on with him. I knew him since Roberto Clemente and ever since I knew him, I associated him with the streets. So me not seeing him, I thought he was in jail or something. I just wanted to know how he was doing. It ain't nothing like that though, I know he got a girl and I got a man. I love Kevin to death. Nothing never happened with me and Love, no kiss, no nothing."

"Oh, aiight, I'm just making sure cuz Marie telling me you asking about him and shit. I just wanted to see what was good cuz it just didn't sound right. I thought I would have to check him or something."

"Oh, Marie was telling you that? That's her in the car?"

"Yeah."

Lenoya walked over to the passenger side of the car and asked, "What's the problem?"

"What's the problem? What you mean what's the problem?" Marie said. She was on the phone with Nisha at the time telling her what was happening and when Lenoya came to the car, she discreetly put Nisha on speakerphone so she could hear what Lenoya was saying.

"You telling your friend I'm asking about Love and it wasn't even like that."

"Nah, I told my brother and he was telling her." As Lani walked around to the driver's side, Marie whispered to Lenoya, "She crazy as hell." Lenoya just looked at Lani.

"Man, that jealousy shit is corney. That shit is childish. That shit ain't nothing but problems yo."

"I'm saying, keep it real, if some chick Kev used to mess with was constantly asking about him, you would think something was up too." Lani added.

"Yeah you right."

"So that was my intentions, just to see what was going on that's all."

"Yeah cuz me and my baby's father just had a fight just now over that trying to make people jealous shit, that shit is no good."

"Yeah aiight, be easy. Don't hurt nobody."

Lani and Marie drove off laughing about the incident. When Marie told Love what happened a couple weeks later, all he could say was, "That shit is fucking embarrassing man."

Lani and Niya were closer than ever around this time. Niya was like a little sister to Lani and she wanted to protect her the best way she could. Since Niya wasn't street smart, Lani would educate her about the streets and niggas, often citing her own experiences. Niya and Lani had many similarities with their lives which was the reason they were so close. Lani often bickered with Niya because she had a boy in her life who she was dealing with for seven years who treated her like shit.

She had been with Trent forever and was never his girlfriend. He basically had his way with her and could fuck her whenever he wanted to. She would fuck other niggas, but whenever he would come back into the picture, it would be fuck whoever she was dealing with. She fucked him whenever he had a girlfriend and never thought anything about what she was doing. But when Lani came along, she told her about herself.

Lani never knew Trent, but from what Niya told her, she knew she wouldn't like him. She even stopped talking to Niya at one point because she still chose to deal with him. He used her and he didn't love her; and Lani had been there, done that already and was never going back. Lani tried to tell Niya that he was never going to do anything with her, especially if he hadn't already. Niya had fucked with a friend of his, so he definitely wasn't going to do anything with her. Niya never listened to Lani though. It was probably because she wanted so much to be loved by Trent. She was naive to the fact that if it hadn't happened in seven years, it was never going to happen. He even had a baby on her. That still didn't stop Niya from catering to his needs though. And when she told Lani she sucked his dick (which she did during their friendship), Lani really washed her hands with her.

She told Lani she only did it out of curiosity and she wanted to know what all the hoopla was about. Lani was upset with her because she told her she should have saved that for someone special, and he definitely was not special. Lani wanted so much for her to leave him alone, but she hadn't learned her lesson that a person is going to do whatever they want to do. Lani had her share of shiesty men and she wanted to educate anyone close to her about signs to look for in men.

Niya was loyal to Lani. She stood by her side through everything and she would break her neck for Lani. Her reasons were mainly because Lani was all she had and she kept it so real with her. Lani didn't tell her what she wanted to hear, but rather her honest opinion about everything. That, in turn, made Niya cling to Lani like mother and child. Right before kidney surgery, Lani found out Niya was pregnant by Trent.

When Lani had her kidney surgery, Love and Niya were there for her; Nisha and Marie also visited her on her last day. As Lani was being transported for the OR to her room, she saw Love and

Niya in the waiting room sitting together talking. She didn't like what she saw and became jealous. Although Niya later told her that Love was saying how much he loved Lani and wanted to grow old with her, she didn't trust what she saw. After what Reasha did, she didn't put anything past a female when it came to her man. Lani didn't want anyone near this man. Although Niya was her friend, she didn't know if deep down inside she wanted what Lani had. She knew how good Love treated her and all the things Lani told her about; for all Lani knew, she had ulterior motives behind her.

While Lani was on bed rest, Niya was the only one who was at her side every single day. If she wasn't there, it was only because she worked all day. She even left work some days to be with her friend. It benefited her too because of the fatigue she suffered from during her pregnancy. That showed Lani that she was down for the cause, and although she had only known her for about a year and a half, it felt like she knew her for ten years.

All of a sudden, Lani was anti-abortion and she tried to tell Niya not to get an abortion. Niya decided she would keep it and Lani was happy. Trent didn't want her to keep the baby though. He had an eight month old and told Niya he wasn't ready for two back to back children. Niya still planned on keeping it, but after she put her thoughts on the table, she decided to get rid of it.

Although Lani threatened she wouldn't talk to Niya anymore if she got the abortion, Niya still went through with it. She still lived home with her mother and didn't have any money for an apartment. Her mother had already made it clear prior to the incident that if she had a baby she had to get her own apartment. She also knew she wouldn't be able to juggle a baby, her shopping habits and bills. After she explained to Lani, "I'm not gonna be able to maintain an apartment and my baby and myself being a waitress at Applebees.

184

Where I'm a live, with you and Love? You gon' let me my baby, you and Love all stay in a one bedroom apartment?" Lani had to let her do what she had to do because Lord knows Lani wasn't letting nobody move in with her.

Months after Niya got the abortion, she would often complain to Lani about pains she would have in her abdomen. Since she didn't have any insurance, she never bothered to check anything out. After a while, she finally decided to check it out. Lani was sad when she heard what happened to her. Niya called Lani crying early in the morning one day. Lani didn't know what to think or what happened, but Niya told her what was going on.

"Lani, you are not going to believe this." Niya said sobbing.

"What, what happened? You okay? Why you crying?"

"I went to the emergency room last night. I couldn't go any longer having these pains in my stomach. Do you know I waited nine hours for them to tell me I have PID (Pelvic Inflammatory Disease)?" Not waiting for a response, Niya quickly added. "Do you know what PID is?"

"Yeah, isn't it when you have multiple sex partners constantly? By having multiple partners and since they have different dick sizes, it does something to your pelvis like shift it or something right?"

"Yeah, that too, but you can also get it when you have untreated STD's. That motherfucker burnt me. And I had to have it for a long time because it turned into PID." Lani's mouth dropped to the floor. For her, it sounded all too familiar. She started thinking back and she was kind of happy Niya got rid of the baby because something may have been wrong with it. She also started thinking back to Niya's risky behavior.

Months prior to her sleeping with Trent again, she had been sleeping with a corney boy Lani went to high school with. After meeting him in a club on New Year's Eve, Niya fucked him two days later. They had a strictly sexual relationship and after only two weeks, she began fucking him raw. Their relationship ended when he just stopped calling.

That made Lani wonder if it was indeed Trent who burnt her. Maybe she burnt Trent. She also was fucking the boy who was one of Trent's friends. She claimed she had been using a condom with him, but she was putting herself at more than STD risk.

"I don't know what I got. They testing the samples and they are gonna call me back with the results. In the meantime, they gave me some medicine to get rid of it." Lani thought for sure that after this, Niya would definitely leave Trent alone. Although Love had burnt her, he never treated her like shit, so their situation was totally different. Lani was able to connect with her empathetically because she knew exactly how she felt. That was the worst feeling in the world, and in her case, she walked around with it for months. Lani knew she felt dirty because that was exactly how she felt.

The next day Niya told Lani she had Chlamydia. And then the day after that, she found out she also had Gonorrhea. Trent or whoever it was, gave her two STD's. She damn sure learned her lesson after that.

She left Trent alone for a few weeks, but then she was right back talking to him and that pissed Lani off more than anything. Niya didn't even mention what he did to her. Lani just left the situation alone and knew eventually she would see the light.

Chapter Thirteen: Moving From Home

Things had gotten crazy in New Haven. Since high school graduation Lani always wanted to leave and experience other cities, but that was just a thought. It didn't become a reality until Lani asked Love if he had a kid in the world.

"I'm sick of this shit Love. I can't do this anymore."

"What are you talking about?"

"Do you have a kid?"

"No, why?"

"Somebody told me you got a kid by somebody. The girl name is Tacarra. They said you had sex with her when you first came home." Tacarra was actually a distant cousin of Lani's whom she didn't talk to.

"Who the hell is Tacarra?" Love asked. "I don't know no damn Tacarra. You think if I had kids I wouldn't know about it. Who wouldn't make it known I'm their baby's father? I'm Love. I got money. I swear on my mother I don't got no kids." Lani believed him, but the look on her face didn't say so and Love recognized that. "You know what, I'm sick of this shit too. We moving out of here. Let's move to Atlanta." Lani never been to Atlanta but heard it was live. She also knew there was a better opportunity there than in her small town. A bigger city meant bigger money in her eyes. There were moves being made in Atlanta and black people were coming up like it was nothing. She wouldn't have any distractions and she

187

would be able to use her ambitiousness to make something happen so she was wit' it.

They were serious about moving. They told people, they visited Atlanta during the fourth of July and they went back again and found an apartment on Lani's birthday. They were definitely moving. They're lease at their current apartment would be up in September so they agreed to move to Georgia in September. Love told Lani he would have 50 G's and would give her ten if only she gave him his space and let him go hard at the streets. She agreed because she had things she needed to do herself and she knew since they were leaving, they could strengthen their relationship.

Before Love left, he promised to make it his business to get his man in jail a better lawyer so he could get an appeal and be released. Being the real man Love was, he donated $15,000 to a new lawyer for his boy. He didn't care if his man didn't win the case; at least he knew he tried to make something happen. Though Lani respected what Love did, she was mad because that money could have been for their moving situation.

At this time, Deshawn had paroled to Marie's house. They were like sisters and brothers and Marie's mother looked at him like a son, so no one minded. Deshawn was always annoying to Marie, Nisha, and Lani. He had changed his life around after he came home from jail and was doing well. He no longer robbed people, but rather this time he got his own money. When he first came home, he had his head on right and got a job and his license. After a while though, he quit his job and became a full-time hustler.

Getting money started to get to his head; he became a wanksta after that. He made it seem like he had so much money and even Love didn't like how he was running around frontin'. He was doing well for himself, but he was blowing it out of proportion. He brought a motorcycle and everytime Lani and Marie would see him and he saw them, he would pop wheelies and ride all wild to show off for them. One particular time, he even pulled out a zip lock bag of money to Love as if to impress him. He knew how Love was doing his thing so he wanted Love to acknowledge him. That didn't impress Love one bit but it was funny to him that he did that.

Deshawn also planted a seed. He had met a bum chick who he got pregnant. He got her pregnant while he had another girlfriend and he offered her a "G" to get rid of it, but she didn't. She figured, *why get a G when I can get more,* so she kept the baby after knowing him for about two months. His baby's mother was also Candy's cousin.

Marie was still involved with Torey while still visiting Mark. Mark heard everything that was going on in the world, including the confrontation between Love and Torey. He didn't like Torey either, so when he heard Love beat him with a bat, he loved it. Though Marie denied cheating with Torey, Mark wasn't stupid. There was even a time when Marie was at Torey's house and a friend of Mark's saw her car parked outside his house. When Marie left in the morning, there was a note on her car which read *I hope you're happy with who you wit'.* The friend then told Mark, but Marie denied it. Lani tried to warn Marie that he wasn't going to do nothing but use her while he was in jail and then shit on her when he got out, but she wanted to see for herself.

Marie also cheated on him with someone else he knew. Marie had a crush on Jamal for the longest and finally got a piece of him. Jamal also knew Love and had been confronted by Love before about his sister – as if he didn't learn already. Since Jamal had a

189

girlfriend, Love didn't want him using Marie for some ass so he wanted to see if he was trying to make something happen.

Marie was wildin' out though. She had confided in Lani that she thought Torey gave her something, but she never got checked. Torey had begun smoking dust at this time and he was still messing with Klarrissa. Oblivious to Mark's feelings in jail or even his abusiveness, Marie was trying to get pregnant by him but after trying and trying, she told Lani she thought he couldn't have kids because he smoked so much. She even took naked pictures for him and left them with him. She asked him about them later on, but he claimed he lost the camera.

The Van Dome was the live club in New Haven to go to on Thursday's. When Keyshia Cole came to the Van Dome two days after her album was released, Lani and Marie had to go. Nisha didn't go because she didn't have anything to wear and her hair wasn't done, so Lani and Marie rolled together. Lani dressed up with her sandals and it was likewise for Marie. The club was packed and Marie and Lani were feeling Keyshia Cole. They were fucked up and into the show. When Remy Martin passed through the crowd, they gave her a hug and gave her her props and told her she was "madd live and doing her thing in the game."

Afterwards was even liver as everyone cruised the after strip. Lani was on the phone telling Nisha how live the show and after strip was when she noticed her female cousin on a motorcycle. Traffic was slow so she walked over to talk to her cousin. While talking to her cousin in the middle of the street, a black SUV rolled up on the opposite side and a female's voice began talking to Lani.

"A, tell her to be careful on that bike." Lani looked in the back seat of the vehicle and saw Keyshia Cole. She quickly ended any conversation between her and her cousin and ran over to the truck while still on the phone with Nisha.

"Yo Keyshia Cole, your album is the shit yo." Lani said, words slurring from the liquor she consumed. "I swear to God you is about to blow. I dedicated number seven to my motherfucking fiancée yo cuz that shit is so real. I feel like packin' up my shit and leaving the engagement ring cuz from the looks of things I can't do this yo." Keyshia Cole just sat there looking at Lani while another occupant of the car was taping her. They were probably thinking, *this damn girl is crazy.*

When they left the club, Nisha blew Torey up but he didn't answer the phone. She wanted to go over his house but when he didn't answer, she had no choice but to go home. When Lani went home, she told Love all about her night. She was still drunk and couldn't go to sleep. After talking to him for about an hour, Lani started telling him about what happened between her and Donell. Love was hurt but he couldn't do anything. She told him she didn't fuck him but told him how close they were but she couldn't do it because she thought about him. It hurt him more that she almost gave his pussy away and it hurt him even more that she could have cheated also. He wanted to get at Donell again for disrespecting him and not caring about the talk they had before; not knowing that the talk came after their rendezvous. He eventually left it alone but was hurt.

The next day morning Lani had been getting blown up by Nisha. She was tired as hell, so she kept ignoring the calls. On her way to work she returned Nisha's call to see what she wanted. "Bitch, have you talked to Marie yet?" Nisha asked.

"No, why, what up?"

"Call her yo, she is wild."

191

"She was mad drunk last night, what did she do?" Lani was thinking all types of thoughts. *I know this chick didn't suck Jamal off. Who did she fight? Who did she catch Torey with?*

"Well, I'm not gonna tell you because it's not my place to tell you. Just call her. She at work so call her and then call me back." *What the hell this girl do that it ain't Nisha's place to tell me? Any other time she tell me shit without her consent,* Lani thought. Lani didn't know what the hell Marie was about to tell her. She called her and when she told her what happened, it was the last thing Lani was thinking.

"What's up yo, what happened last night?" Lani asked.

"Oh, you talked to Nisha?" Marie responded.

"Yeah, and she said something happened last night. What's good homey?"

"Oh, so she didn't tell you nothing?" Marie asked laughing.

"No, she told me you should be the one to tell me."

Marie laughed and whispered, "Lani, I humped Shawn." Lani's mouth fell right to the floor. She was absolutely speechless. At that point, she was convinced there was no such thing as men and women friendships; she began to acknowledge Mark because he had been right about a lot of shit so far.

"Oh, my God. How the hell did that happen?"

"It's all Torey's fault. If he would have just answered, it would have never happened."

"Okay, how did that happen?"

"Well when I got home, I kept calling Torey. When he didn't answer, I went downstairs to talk to Shawn and see if he knew why Torey wasn't answering. I was drunk and I kept messing with him. Next thing I knew he started kissing me."

"And you didn't stop huh?"

192

"No, I was horney girl. If I wasn't drunk I probably would have stopped him but I don't know. After we were done, I realized what I did and ran upstairs to my room and closed the door. But why when I was on the way up the stairs, my mother was standing at the top of the stairs and asked me what I was doing. You think she knew?"

"I don't know, but you know if she did she would have spoke on it, you know your mother crazy. But just tell me did ya'll use one?"

Marie started laughing and answered, "No." Lani just shook her head in awe. *Damn, I hope Torey didn't give her anything. She never got checked so I hope she not passing nothing or she gon' be cheap. She don't want to be the one passing nothing. That shit ain't cute. At least if she was gonna get somethin', be the one getting, not givin'. That shit is embarrassing,* Lani thought. "He called here today and I ignored all his calls. I don't know what to say. I really don't want it to happen again. I finally answered and he was like 'Yo, don't tell nobody what happened. We gotta take this to our graves yo, word up.' I agreed with him but then he was like 'I'm sayin' though, that shit was kinda right.' Why he say that Lani?"

"I don't know. Ya'll niggas crazy. I can't believe you did Shawn, yo. That is one aggravating motherfucker and I never looked at him like that. Last night was wild anyway. I was drunk and you were even drunker. I was so drunk, I slipped and told your brother about what almost happened between me and Donell."

"Okay…Why did you do that? You told him everything?"

"Yeah, but that's what he get. He need to know I'm capable of cheating too. I feel better knowing I told him anyway just in case he ever heard it on the street."

"You didn't tell him I knew though right?"

"No, I didn't mention anything about you."

193

"Oh, good cuz I hope he don't come asking me nothing cuz I don't know nothing. I'ma say I didn't have any idea about that because I don't want him thinking I'm shiesty for not telling him."

"Well he's dumb if he think you would tell him anyway. I think he already know you wouldn't tell him if I was cheating. But he know you would tell me if he was cheating."

"Yeah you right, because he is a nigga and niggas do chicks dirty and I could not sit here and know my friend is being played. But if you was playing him, shit, he a nigga, he could deal with it. But what I'm gonna do about Shawn?"

"Just act normal yo, and ya'll cannot do it again. He has a girlfriend and you don't want that drama again. Shit starting to die down and you know she Candy cousin so you know she would get involved again right? If Mark knew, you know he would automatically think ya'll been fucking right?"

"Yeah I know, tell me about it girl."

"And ya'll need to be using rubbers. Ya'll niggas crazy. So what ya'll knew each other for years, you don't know what that girl got and didn't you say she was a hoe?"

"Yeah, I know. I don't want it to happen again." Although Marie said she didn't want it to happen anymore, that wasn't the last time.

Things began to go bad between Lani and Love again. They were arguing every other day, Lani was sleeping on the couch every other night, and they were close to breaking up for good. Love began partying every week and Lani didn't agree with that because he had a mission to complete; he had to move as much work as he could in a few months, and he wasted time by going to the club. She

194

told him about himself every time and he disagreed; that pushed them apart.

It took Lani about six months to fully get over Love cheating on her; though she never fully got over it. No one gets over someone cheating on them completely, and how could you? Occasionally when you get into those moods and look at the motherfucker, you can't help but think how he (or she) fucked someone else. You know that person is capable of doing it again if they did it once, so out of nowhere you release anger towards them. So you never really forget what they did. But during her time of mourning, Lani managed to annoy Love, Marie, and Nisha about the girl. She never got to see how she looked and she humiliated herself. She gained some trust for Love, but she still thought he would cheat on her again. She pushed him away so much, he began to not care about the relationship anymore and he began showing signs that he was cheating again.

Luckily Donell went back to jail before the incident happened or Lani would have fucked him and thought nothing of it. She did have a crush on a cute boy from the "Ville." He didn't hustle but he hung in the streets. Brian was blazin and every girl wanted him. He was about six feet tall, light-skinned and had pretty hair. Lani had seen him around before, but she didn't think he paid her any attention. She flirted with him a few times after Love cheated on her and he wanted her too but he was too fine to show it. Other than him, there was no one else she was interested in having sex with, so she needed a way to let him know she could cheat too; so she made him think it.

She began coming in the house late and she kept her feet done and appearance totally up to par. She didn't talk to him much, she didn't call him throughout the day, and she didn't answer when

195

he called. She also kept her phone off all night. He began to think she was cheating.

About two months after the incident that happened with Love and Torey, Marie and Love were speaking again. So around this time, Love would call Marie to tell her he thought Lani was cheating. Marie knew about Lani's plan and would simply say, 'that girl ain't cheating.' Love didn't agree though. His proof (or so he thought) finally came when Lani planted a condom in her pocket. She left her pants on the floor and positioned the condom as if it fell out her pocket unintentionally. Love found the condom the next morning while she was in the shower. He burst into the bathroom while she was singing Keyshia Cole's song, "I Should've Cheated," and said, "What the fuck is this?" with the condom in his hand. Lani looked at the condom, paused for a few to laugh in her head, and gave answers only a man would.

"It's a condom. Is that yours?"

"No, I found it in your pants pocket on the floor."

"What?" Lani said, knowing exactly what he said but she needed time to get her thoughts together.

"You heard me. It was on the floor hanging out your pants pocket."

"Oh, that's Nisha's. I had took it out her car. I intended to throw it away, but accidentally put it in my pockets." That was definitely something a man would say, always blaming it on the friend.

"Yeah right." Love just looked at her in disbelief and went into the living room to iron his clothes. When Lani got out the shower, she went in the living room to talk to him. She rubbed his side and all of a sudden, he bolted into the bedroom and laid on the bed face down and began crying.

196

"Stop it with your fake cries." Lani said. She knew he wasn't really crying. He turned over and had a few tears coming down. "What is wrong with you?" Lani asked.

"Cause I know you cheating on me." Lani was glad her plan worked. *Yeah motherfucker, now you know exactly how it feel*, Lani thought in her head. She had no remorse for his feelings. She wanted him to think someone else wanted his gir and she was willing to play it out to the endl.

"Baby, I'm not cheating on you." Lani said.

"Who is he?"

"Who is who, you?"

"I'ma find out who he is. I ain't gon' call numbers back, but I'ma investigate."

"Well go ahead. Good Luck."

"I'ma beat the nigga ass too. Ain't nobody taking my girl away from me. I know I did wrong and I probably deserve this, but whatever you doing, just please stop." Lani was at ease. Her plan worked perfectly. He could investigate all he wanted and would find nothing. He really did investigate too, that is, until Marie snitched on Lani.

Marie told Love Lani planted the condom and she wanted him to think she was cheating. Marie claimed he was whining to her so she felt she should have just told him. Lani was highly upset because that was her man and if she wanted him to think she was cheating, that was her business, but that was her fault for involving people in her business anyway. Lani told Love Marie was lying, and he would be a fool to believe her. She was able to convince him she was lying stating, "why would I plant a condom?"

After that, Love paid more attention to Lani and her needs; he was the man he was when he came home. He loved "his queen" and didn't want to lose her. Things got better, and then just like that they got worse, AGAIN.

They say when you're trying to get out the ghetto, you should just leave and don't tell anybody because no one wants to see you doing good. That statement couldn't have meant more sense to Lani after she had a life changing situation.

Love disregarded Lani's requests and continued to party. He wanted to leave her so bad, but he couldn't get his heart back. He tried to force her to leave by continuously going out, but the last night he went out was probably his most regretful adventure.

The night Lani didn't have her gun almost cost her her life or it may have saved her from dying; you be the judge. Since Love was on a clubbin' spree, he wasn't able to protect her the night she was robbed. She hadn't talked to him that whole day because of a disagreement they had the night before. She had no idea where he was, but she knew he wouldn't be home until late just to make her angrier.

She pulled into her apartment complex around ten thirty at night and parked in her usual parking space. As she was parking, she noticed a white Chevy Lumina with limo tinting already parked in the area she normally parked in. There wasn't anything suspicious about the vehicle; she just never saw it in the complex before. She didn't think anything of it because she lived in a suburban area so she figured it was a visitor or occupant of the complex. She was returning from the store so she had her hands full while walking in the house. She didn't grab her pistol located under her seat because she had her hands full. As she walked to her apartment's side entrance, she heard doors slam behind her. She turned around to

198

see two men dressed in black with masks on running towards her. One man poked her with the gun and ordered her to open the door.

"Open the door right now. If you scream I will kill you." Lani was petrified. She had never been robbed before. She had no idea who the men were or what they were looking for. She opened the door while crying. "Where's your boyfriend?" One of the men asked.

"I don't know." Lani said.

"Where the money at?"

"What money, I don't know." The man pushed Lani to the ground, cocked his gun back and said, "you think we fucking playing? Where's the money?" Unlike Love, Lani didn't believe it was worth dying over material things. She felt if you got it once, you could get it again.

"Okay." Lani said. "It's in the bedroom." Lani got off the floor and walked to the bedroom while she had a gun in her back. She wished Love was there to save her. When she got in the room, they pushed her on the bed. One held the gun to her while the other searched the room.

"Now where is it?"

"He usually keeps everything in the drawer." Lani showed the men the drawers he kept his money and product in. The men gathered everything and gained a total of about twenty thousand in drugs and money altogether. The men were greedy so they knew that wasn't it.

"Where's the rest of it?" The man asked, tearing the room apart.

"I don't know, that's all I know. He don't keep everything here." Lani refused to tell them where Love kept his safe, which was in the closet under clothes. She told them enough so if they found the safe, it would be their luck. The man opened the closet and

199

began tearing it apart. The safe was at the bottom of the closet. Since the man was tall, he went for the top shelves first. God must have been with her because all of a sudden the man in the closet received a call. She heard him say "okay" and told the other man they had to leave. They left and Lani laid there for about a minute in shock, still crying. Those were the longest five minutes of her life.

She jumped up, ran out the door and drove out her complex. She tried to reach Love on both cell phones to tell him what happened, but he didn't answer. He probably thought she wanted to argue or pick a fight. She knew he was at the club because his money phone was off. She thought he was out with one of his friends whom Marie talked to, so she called Marie to get Jamal's number. Marie didn't notice anything suspicious with her, so she gave the number.

Jamal wasn't with Love but he told her he was in Hartford at the club and didn't know who he was with. He heard Lani crying and called Love to tell him Lani was looking for him, then he called Marie to see what was going on. Love called her back and began yelling at her. "What the fuck is wrong with you calling other people looking for me?"

"While you were out partying, your fucking crib was getting robbed." Lani yelled angrily.

"What?"

"Your fucking crib just got robbed." She said even louder.

"Lani whatever, it's over with okay. It's over."

"Are you not hearing me? Your fucking crib just got robbed."

"It's over with, goodbye." Love didn't believe her. After he hung up with her, Marie called her back because she was with Love and overheard what he was saying.

200

"Don't involve me in that bullshit between you and my brother. I shouldn't have given you Jamal's number." Lani was furious because Marie had no idea what was going on. She also didn't know Marie was with Love at the club so she heard what Love was saying. Lani just blacked out on Marie.

"Fuck you and your brother. I just got guns pointed to my head and that's all ya'll can say. Fuck ya'll."

All Lani heard Marie say was, "Oh my god are you serious," before she hung up. Love and Marie left the club after that and drove home. They were in Hartford, which was about a half an hour from where Lani was. Lani waited in the parking lot of a hotel close to where she lived. She waited about an hour and hadn't received a call from Love. She decided to go back home and upon her arrival, she saw his car there. When she went in the house, he was on the phone.

She walked in with her gun in her hand. When she walked in, she heard him say to the person on the phone, "Oh, now she got her gun in her hand." And he chuckled. Lani had an indescribable anger at that point. She didn't say anything to Love. He thought she was playing a joke on him to get him home. It wasn't that serious though because just as much as he wasn't feeling her at the time prior to this, she wasn't feeling him the same. They both wanted to leave each other, but they both knew they would find no one like the other. Besides, if it was a game, she would have come clean when he got home.

They began arguing. Love was lying on the bed yelling at her. He thought it was a hoax because the robbers didn't get the safe with the real money in it. After about three minutes of arguing, he finally said, "I'm straight, I don't need a girl if I'm gonna have to deal with shit like this."

201

No one could imagine how she felt. She combined all her anger and responded, "You straight, you straight. I got robbed and you straight on me? Fuck you." Out of nowhere she punched him in the face with all her strength. He grabbed her, threw her on the bed and held her arms down with his knees and starting slapping her in the face like she was a man. He wasn't fighting fair. Lani couldn't defend herself. She yelled at him for him to let her go.

"You calm now, you calmed down now?"

"Yup, I'm calm." Lani said. He let her go and she punched him again. "Don't be fucking hitting me like that." Lani cried. He grabbed her, threw her to the floor and hit her more. When she finally got back up, she went to the living room and grabbed her gun, cocked it back and went back to the bedroom. She just stood there silently with the gun to her side.

"Oh, what I'm supposed to be scared now cuz you got your little gun? Shoot me. You better kill me." Lani couldn't do it. If it wasn't for the thought of being in jail for life, she would have killed him at that moment because of the way she was feeling. Although she may have gotten off for acting in self defense and she had a legal gun, she still couldn't do it. Love went to the bathroom to wipe the blood off his face and prepared to leave. While in the bathroom, Lani hid her gun under the couch just in case it got serious and decided to kill her, grabbed a butcher knife and headed out the door to flatten his tires. Love grabbed her before she could walk out, took the knife out her hands and the fighting resumed. He got her to the ground, held her hands together with one of his hands, and beat the left side of her face. She laid there unconscious and gasping for oxygen. She cried and screamed hysterically. He tried to calm her down and he thought he almost killed her. He told her she was too loud and someone would call the police. He asked her did she want

202

him to go to jail. After she didn't stop her cries, he grabbed his safe and ran out the door.

After Lani laid there for about two more minutes, she, too, left. As she drove out the complex, she was stopped by Marie and Deshawn entering the complex. Marie got out the car and approached Lani in her car. When Marie saw Lani's face, she was shocked. Lani had a black eye and her cheek was swollen with scratches all over her left side. Marie didn't know what to do, and there was nothing she could do. Lani explained everything that happened and was able to convince Marie she was telling the truth. Marie tried to convince Love but she had no luck. Lani threatened to kill herself right there because Love didn't believe her. She grabbed her gun and Marie was scared. She tried to take the gun from her, but Lani refused. Marie did not want Lani to drive off by herself with the gun. She couldn't live with that on her conscience knowing she could have prevented tragedy. After an unsuccessful struggle, Marie just said fuck it and she and Deshawn drove over to the hotel with Lani to make sure she was straight. Even Deshawn tried to take the gun from Lani, but she again refused. After she checked into the hotel, Marie called Lani's mother and told her what was going on.

Lani hadn't talked to her mother in weeks prior to this incident. She was very upset that Marie told her mother what happened, especially since she had every intention on telling her the next day; less the threats to kill herself. Aside from that, Lani felt it wasn't her place to tell her mother anything. Even if she was only calling her to tell her Lani said she would kill herself, if Lani really wanted to do it, there was nothing her mother could have done because she wasn't in front of her. As Lani always stated, "nobody should be calling my mother to tell her anything unless I'm dead or injured." Her mother went off on her on her voicemail since she didn't answer but that only added to Lani's anger.

Over the next few days, Love slandered Lani's name. He had all his family and friends thinking she lied about the robbery. He told them she hit him and pulled a gun out on him. From then, Lani began to see the true colors come out in some people. Everybody who adored her prior to that immediately shunned her. They told Love he didn't need to be with her anyway, she was young and he deserved better, leave her alone, all types of things and they hadn't heard Lani's side of the story. She felt if they were so quick to say that, then they felt that way all along. Lani felt very lonely. She had no one to confide in but Niya.

After Love talked to Lani's mom to cover himself about hitting on her, Lee flipped on Lani. She never really mentioned the robbery. She was more concerned with why Lani threatened to kill herself than the robbery. She also wanted her and Love to work their problems out and stay together. After they argued back and forth, Lani's mother told her to get her things from her house before dark and move back in with her until they left. Lani followed her mom's wishes and did just that.

It had been two days since the robbery. Lani hadn't spoken with Love and she felt he calmed down by now. She didn't care if they never got back together she just wanted to prove herself. She called him and he was interested in talking to her. He expressed sorrow for putting his hands on her and told her he missed her. He asked if he could see her and they met up at a Walgreen's store. He hadn't seen her since he beat her up (unfairly) and when he saw her, he was hurt. Her face was still swollen and eye still discolored.

They talked in the car for a few and Lani told him what happened. He believed her and expressed more sorrow. He felt like

204

an idiot. They didn't break up, but they had a lot of things to work on, especially if they planned on getting married. He vowed that he would make one more trip to New York and they would move to Atlanta when he sold the last of his drugs. Since he took a major loss, he was unable to move the amount of work he wanted to, but decided to leave with whatever he had when the time came.

Things got better over the next few weeks between Lani and Love. They didn't argue and Love was kissing her ass more than ever because he felt guilty. He couldn't erase that night, but he damn sure wanted to make up for it. He tried to find out who did the robbery because he wanted to retaliate. Lani didn't want him to because she put it in the hands of the Lord and she didn't want to see anything happen to him in the process. She was still alive so she wasn't stressing the issue as much. She didn't want Love to be behind bars for something he could get back if he was out, but it was a man thing.

He investigated the robbery thoroughly. He had his cousin, D, as a suspect because he was the only one he ever brought to his house. He didn't think anyone else knew where he lived; he thought it was an inside job. He was unsuccessful in his quest. About three weeks after the robbery however, Love received word from jail that Torey was up there bragging about his part in the robbery. He had been arrested again for violation of probation about two weeks after the robbery. He picked Lani up from work and was telling her what happened.

"Yo, I know who was behind that too."

"Okay...Who?" Lani's heart dropped.

"That bitch ass nigga Torey. And I swear I started thinking he had something to do with it. After I eliminated D, he was the only one who could have had something to do with it. My mans and them

205

called me from jail and told me he up there bragging about the shit. They said he even said something like, 'Yeah, his girl always pulling guns out on him'. How he even know about some damn guns being pulled out...my sister. And he was like, he better watch his girl."

"First of all, what the hell that supposed to mean? Is he trying to say I had something to do with it too?"

"I don't know bay, this is what I was told."

"He don't need to try to involve me in nothing cuz he can't try and make me look bad. I ain't guilty about shit so he can go ahead with that bullshit. He just trying to make both our lives miserable cuz he miserable. And pulling guns out, first of all, it was only that one time I pulled the damn gun out on you. That's some fucking bullshit and he is a bitch ass nigga for that shit man."

Love was livid. After analyzing the situation, he thought Marie told Torey they went to the club that night. He decided to talk to Marie one last time to let her know what was going on and hopefully get her to tell the truth. She broke down and told him she did tell him they were going out, but she didn't have any cruel intentions behind mentioning that. She didn't think he knew where they lived and she didn't think he would violate his curfew (he was on the bracelet at the time). Love also talked to his sister in an effort to point out how she was used and abused and how the dude wasn't shit. She still continued to deal with him despite this and in return lost her brother, FOREVER. Lee couldn't understand why Lani still dealt with Marie since she chose to still deal with Torey. She felt if she still dealt with him after everything that happened, Marie didn't care about Lani. Lani loved Marie like a sister, even before Love came in the picture, and she honestly believed Marie didn't mean any harm in the situation; her only anger came when she still chose to deal with Torey.

Torey was a sucker, cornball ass nigga. He waited until he got to jail to say he did it. Real niggas would have waited in the house until Love got home, not got his girl. Love beat his ass with a bat and he went after his girlfriend, not him. He was a lame ass dude for that. Lani never thought of him as a suspect because she didn't think he knew where they lived. She also would have known he was one of them because of his distinguished walk he acquired from being shot; but he could have been the caller. He should have made himself known. He waited until he got in police custody to start singing. He got no props for that and Lani told Love not to waste his time on the bum, he would get his. Love agreed, saying Torey was the type to sign statements on him and he did four years behind someone like him.

The night before Lani left, Marie and Nisha took her out to Humprey's. As they were sitting chillin', they began talking to one of Brian's friends. While they were talking to Jamar, Brian was walking along side the building and they all saw him coming in.

"Lani, Lani, look who coming in." Lani looked out the window and saw Brian coming in. She began fixing herself up, as if she wasn't already presentable enough. She was well dressed for her last evening and wanted to be remembered as the little fly murda mami.

She was definitely noticed by Brian. She had on a green lacoste v-neck sweater which exposed her chest just a little. She had on denim blue lacoste jeans with the alligators' body equally stitched on the back pockets, drawing attention to her nice sized ass. To finish the outfit, she had on black suede Prada sneakers.

When Brian came in, he walked over to the table and sat in the vacant seat; which just so happened to be next to Lani. "Yo, he is

207

blazin Lani, you need to tear that up. It's your last night here and you might not never get the chance to get a piece of that." Nisha said.

"Yeah I know, he look right tonight. He got on my man jeans too. My man got those jeans." Lani added with a smirk.

"A Brian you know tonight Lani's last night here right?" Marie said.

"Oh word, where you going?" Brian asked as if concerned.

"I'm moving to Atlanta." Lani replied shyly.

"Oh the A-town huh? You going far. I couldn't go that far."

"Give her a hug." Marie instigated. Brian gave Lani a hug, making her blush. She felt like a little kid as if she was in high school and had a crush. He definitely made her night with that.

As the night went on, Brian and his friend would leave the restaurant. As Lani and her friends were on their way out the door, Jamar called Marie back. He told her to wait at the restaurant; Jamar left his car and hopped in the car with Brian so they wanted to see them when they got back. When they got back to the restaurant, they all were outside reminiscing on past events. Marie and Nisha were in the front seat of Marie's car while Lani was in the back. Brian and Jamar were outside the car. After persuading him, Marie got Brian to sit in the back with Lani. She had been instigating something between them the whole night, and Lani didn't stop her. As they were about to pull off, Marie added, "Yo Brian, you should give Lani a ride home."

"Why, ya'll not bringin' me home?"

"No, we gotta do something right quick. Brian gon' bring you home right." *What these bitches gotta do that they can't involve me in? They not slick at all.* Lani thought.

"Yeah, I'll bring her home if she want me to." Brian got out the car and walked over to say goodbye to Jamar. While in the car Marie

208

and Nisha edged Lani on to go with him. Lani eventually did as she wanted to tell him how she felt before she left; she didn't know if she would ever see him again.

While they drove, he never asked her where she lived. She noticed him driving toward the "Ville" which was where he lived. As he drove by the Jump, she asked him where he was going. He told her he just wanted to cruise the after strip of the Jump but he was on the way to his house until Lani stopped him. She then made him bring her to Nisha's house since she and Love stayed at her mother's house (since Lee now knew him, he was able to stay with Lani now – with the door open) and she didn't want to be in the car with him and Love catch her. They parked at Nisha's house and started talking.

"So this is it huh?" Lani asked.

"Yeah. You about to go far away."

"Yeah. I need to get away from here. Ain't nothing here but bullshit, you know."

"Yeah, but I ain't never leaving here. All my niggas here man." As they talked for a few more minutes, Love was blowing Lani up. She kept ignoring his calls and continued talking to Brian.

As Lani was saying goodbye to Brian, she gave him a hug, opened the car door and said, "So I guess I'm never gonna be able to do what I wanted to do with you," and closed the door and continued walking.

He rolled the window down and responded, "Wait, hold up, what you wanted to do." He knew exactly what she was talking about but wanted to hear it from her mouth. She got back in the car and sat in the back seat so she couldn't look at him directly.

"You know what I'm talking about."

"No I don't. Say what you mean. All you gotta do is say it. I ain't gonna bite." Lani sat there going back and forth with him for about four minutes. *Damn Lani, have an affair, act like an adult for once. You not gon' never be able to see this nigga ever again,* Lani thought. She finally got the balls to say what was on her mind.

"I'm sayin', you know I always wanted to fuck you right."

"C'mon, we could be out right now." Brian said without a fight.

"It's not that easy though. I want to real bad but I'm scared..." Before Lani gave him a chance to think she was either scared that he would break her back or something like that, she added, "I'm scared to cheat."

"Oh, yeah, I can't say nothing about that. That's serious. I'm gonna leave that up to you. All you gotta do is say the word though and we could be out right now."

Lani looked at her phone as Love's name flashed across her screen. While looking at her phone, she said, "Well you gon' be up in about a half an hour?"

"I don't know, I'm tired but you can try." Lani took Brian's number and told him if she called that meant he could come and get her. She got out the car and called Nisha and Marie to come and get her.

When Nisha and Marie arrived, they were eager to know why she called them so quick. "Damn, what happened? I know he wasn't that quick." Nisha asked.

"Nah, ain't nothing happened, we was just talking, but why when we first pulled off, he was just about to bring me to his house. He didn't ask me or nothing, he was just about to bring me. He rode by the Jump and when I told him I didn't live over there, he tried to play it off like he was just riding the after strip."

Nisha and Marie chuckled at Lani's statement. "Yeah we know, when ya'll pulled off, Jamar came to the car and told us he told Brian to take you home and blow your back out." Marie told Lani.

"Are you serious?"

"Yeah, that's what they were talking about."

"Well I could have tapped that cuz he was ready and willing. At least I know I'm appealing enough to him, that's good enough."

"So...what was the problem?" Marie and Nisha asked simultaneously.

"I told him I was scared."

Nisha and Marie burst out laughing with amusement. "What the hell were you scared of bitch?" Marie asked.

"I don't want to cheat. I would feel so guilty. Love was calling me and shit. I can't fuck Brian and then go home and look at him."

"Yeah, I feel you. But you stupid as fuck. That nigga is right. You was supposed to put it on him." Nisha said.

"Yeah I know, but I'm glad I didn't. I know he cheated but two wrongs don't make a right. At least I got to tell him how I feel so when I come up to visit, it will give him something to think about. Me doing that only made him want me more, you feel me. It's a chase for him. But if I didn't have Love...O, it would have been on."

"You still stupid."

"It's all good. Take me home please."

Marie and Nisha said their last goodbyes and told Lani they would miss her. Before departing, Nisha gave Lani a few words of advice. "Make sure you stay on top of your shit down there cuz them bitches in Atlanta be fly. So stay on top of your game girl." They hugged and neither of them knew it would be their last time seeing each other.

Lani went home to Love who was in the bed waiting for her. She was glad she didn't cheat on him and then had to go home to look at him. She wouldn't have been able to jump in the shower when she got home or that would have been suspicious or what if he wanted to do her right after; that just wouldn't have been right.

The next day when she woke up, she texted Brian. The text read, *You lucky I got a man or it would have been on. I know you not used to females turning you down, but I bet you not getting none of this only made you want me even more. I don't have this ring on my finger for nothing, remember that. I'm glad you know how I feel though. You never know what will happen in the future. Just save me a piece of that for the next time you see me. One!*

Love and Lani moved to Atlanta in October 2005. They no longer dealt with the bullshit in Connecticut. New Haven was becoming too rough anyway. It was the home that received national attention after some young boys went on a shooting spree targeting innocent people; it was compared to the DC snipper. It was also a place rapper Cassidy performed and was punched in the face by an ignorant young man. They left it all behind though. Out of sight; out of mind. He would be making a way for himself while the lame dudes would be back home flipping 3.5 grams. He decided to leave the drug game alone, become a working man, live a normal life, but of course pursue other, more legitimate hustles.

That was probably the best decision they ever made. Love changed Lani's life from the day she met him. Because of the way he made her look at life and herself, he made her a stronger woman. Just as equally, she showed him the value of being out and able to raise a family, make money, be successful and knowledgeable, rather than wasting years behind bars. She also made him understand it wasn't about being brave or being classified as a sucker, but one must know what things are worth a reaction and what are worth nothing. Despite all the bad things they did to one another, they were both made for each other and no matter what they did, no one would be better for either of them. Their next goal was to get everything together in their new state, a thousand miles from home, and not look back.

They had a lot of memories in New Haven though. Not just together, but even before they met each other. Both had become susceptible to the streets and he lost his mother at an early age. Lani had her trials and tribulations and so did he. Together, they experienced a lot of firsts. They both shared love for the first time. They both shared their first apartment together. They both visited Atlantic City together for the first time. They also shared their first STD together. They also taught each other things the other didn't know. They definitely loved each other and now they were leaving what they knew behind to start something new.

On the ride down south, they decided to stop in Maryland to see Lani's father. He had been living there for about five years and her brother stayed with him while he attended college. She hadn't talked to her father since her senior year in high school and with the help of her brother, she wanted to surprise him. She didn't want to see him because she loved him, but rather she wanted to see him because she wanted to show him she turned out fine without him.

During their encounter, he was able to meet her future husband. He was probably shocked to see she had a real man on her shoulder. He tried to show off and front like he was this big time guy because he worked for Dell and his wife was a loan officer; not realizing that Lani knew everything he had was behind his wife. He told Lani how beautiful she had grown up to be and he loved her. Lani knew that was bullshit because anybody who loves somebody doesn't treat them the way he treated her. Before they left, he told them he would pay for their wedding and also be the Deejay there.

213

That made Lani even angrier because he was talking out his ass. He hadn't even talked to her in years, or seen her, so what the hell made him think she would believe he would pay for her wedding. After that, Lani never wanted to see him ever again. He was a deadbeat not even worth anything to show off to. Shit, he was lucky she didn't pull his card and tell him she heard he was down in Maryland fucking men. He had no idea the resentment Lani had against him as he was never there to save her from anything. Though she didn't blame for any decisions she made in her life, she knew had he been in her life, she would have made better ones.

Chapter Fourteen: The End

Moving to Atlanta was probably the best thing Lani and Love could have done for themselves at the time. They were in a new city where they didn't know anyone; which meant they could be more focused on what they needed to do to become established. Love pursued his mission to become a working man. He didn't want to live the street life anymore, he just wanted to become legit and live like the average man. They were really on another level and they did not have New Haven, Connecticut on their minds.

Things didn't get off to a great start when they arrived to Georgia. They didn't receive their furniture until two weeks after they arrived and they had given the movers their furniture three weeks before they left. Before Lani left, she made sure she would be able to transfer to another Applebees down there, and when she visited months prior, she paid a visit to the location she wanted to transfer to and spoke with the manager. They told her she would be able to transfer, so when she got down there, she did have a job. The first night she worked, she realized just how much she no longer wanted to be in the restaurant business. As a waitress, she made $2.75 an hour plus tips, compared to $5.02 an hour in Connecticut.

When she arrived and was introduced to her co-workers, the manager kept referring to her as the girl from Connecticut; which created ill feelings toward her from the females who worked there. That wasn't the reason for her frustration though. She was sick of being at work forever and not knowing when exactly she would get off. And she also didn't like the fact that when it was time for her to get off, she couldn't just walk out the door; she had to do extra shit. After the first night, she quit and did not go back.

Finding a job was hard for Love and Lani initially. Lani didn't think finding a job for herself would be so hard because she had a solid resume and she didn't have any felonies. She knew it would be difficult for Love because he had a felony, and although his felony was almost nine years old, it still appeared on his criminal record. She tried to tell him to get his CDL license and become a truck driver. Not only was the pay good, but he would be able to do what he did back at home – drive around and get paid. The school was only three weeks, but he didn't take heed to it and still continued to search for a regular job. The jobs they did see paid well under what any of them were used to back at home. They definitely were not used to the south and they both soon became annoyed.

Although they went down south with enough money to hold them over for a few months, without money coming in, they began to see their stacks get smaller and smaller. As a man, Love began to become depressed and wanted to go back home; he started feeling like less of a man and he began missing the fast money he was getting in the streets. They were both survivors and they both knew how to hustle, so they knew if worst came to worst, they would do what they did best – hustle.

Lani did get another job about a month and a half after she quit her first job. She thought the job was sweet because in the interview, the owner told her she would make a minimum of $75,000 a year whether she wanted to or not. That included a weekly pay of about $1000 (depending on how she did) plus bonuses. Unfortunately, it was a commission only job selling health and life insurance. After putting in hours and not making any money, she

216

quit the job after only two weeks. Two months after moving, they both did get jobs.

Love had a job working third shift 6 p.m. until 6 a.m. four days a week. He was making $11 an hour and with eight hours of overtime per week, he was bringing home about a "G" every two weeks. Compared to the streets, that was definitely a pay cut for him considering he made that just about every day. Compared to the first few jobs he had, it was a pay increase. Lani had a job working at Home Depot making $8.50 an hour, which was definitely a pay cut for her but with no money coming in, she had to take what came to her. That provided her with $1200 a month and luckily she wasn't on her own because if she were, she would have been making $1200 a month with $1500 a month in bills. Frustrated with settling with that kind of money, she decided to go back to school so she wouldn't settle for jobs making $10 an hour and shit. She went back to school for Business Management/Marketing at the University of Phoenix in Gwinett County of Georgia. It was definitely an adjustment for them and over time they adapted to the south; but they ultimately decided they would return up north to North Jersey or New York in a couple of years. They were too used to the fast life and style of the northeastern part of the country.

They made the best of their move but they didn't do much. Occasionally they would go to the movies or do something with Love's uncle and cousin, but for the most part, they stayed in the house. Love didn't want to go to the club because being that he thought he was P.Diddy or somebody, he didn't like going to clubs with $20 in his pockets. He wanted to be a baller and pop bottles and shit like that. When he was home, he would go to the clubs or events with custom made leathers, custom made kicks, custom made linen suits, gators, coogis, all types of shit and pop bottles of

Moet, Cristal, whatever, just to show off. Lani on the other hand, didn't mind going to a club with $20. When she was home and would go to the Van Dome, $20 got her in and two drinks plus a tip. That didn't mean she didn't have money though, she just felt that the club was not a place she wanted to spend $200 at; if anything, she would rather spend that kind of money on an outfit to wear to the club.

Weeks after Love cheated on Lani when they were home, she had decided she would write a book on her life. She began writing the book weeks after he cheated on her in March 2005. She had been writing in the book faithfully up until she had kidney surgery and lost interest after that. With nothing else to do and no money coming in, she decided to pursue her book again. She constantly told Love the book would be their million dollar ticket and if she made it, he would make it too. She was serious about that and she was determined to never again be in the financial state she was in. She envisioned her success and in turn made her even more motivated. She vowed that the first half a million she got, she would invest seventy-five percent of it in real estate to ensure she would never be broke again in life.

Love believed in Lani, but he wasn't a true believer. He wasn't as enthusiastic as Lani, probably because he couldn't see the vision as she could. She could see Vibe magazine doing a spread on her. She could see herself being on various talk shows, she could see movie deals coming her way and if not, she could see herself with rental properties generating a total income of $8000 a month. On the luxurious side, she could see herself in that new BMW M6 burgungy with cream leather and burgundy piping driving through her home town with lightly tinted windows so they could see who in it and making motherfuckers sick. With his lifestyle and yearning to be in the spotlight, Love could see himself in one of those too, but with the top down. When she started talking like that, that's when he started pushing her more to pursue her dreams.

Just when things were going good with them, they hit rock bottom. As Lani was cleaning up the house one day, she went to pick up Love's pants and a piece of paper dropped out his pocket. She picked the paper up and it was his time card from work. On one of the days, Friday, the day before New Year's Eve, he clocked out at 1:30 a.m.. Since it was a habit that Lani looked at her clock every time Love came in from work, she knew he was not home at 2:00 that night, more like 3:30. Since he was sleep, she did not wake him up. Instead, she went on about her business and waited for him to call her.

When he called her, she calmly asked him about the situation. "Yo, bay, why you didn't wake me up for work?" Love asked, accustomed to Lani always waking him up.

"Because…you grown, you can get up on your own."

"Damn, where that come from?"

"Nah, I'm saying, you grown, you can get up on your own, you don't need me."

"Oh, alright then. I'll holla at you later cuz you acting funny."

"Nah, I'm not acting funny. I just want you to tell me what's going on."

"What you mean what's going on?"

"You have something to tell me?"

"No. Why you say that?"

"I'm sayin', I was cleaning up and I picked up your pants and saw your time card. You got off at one thirty Friday."

"Okay and?"

"And, so where were you?"

"I dropped my man off who work with me and we had a few drinks since it was the night before New Year's Eve."

"Oh okay." Lani said accepting his answer.

"But hold up. What the fuck you doin' goin' through my stuff anyway?"

"Nobody was going through your stuff. I told you I was cleaning up and the paper fell out your pocket."

"Okay well even if it came out my pocket, the paper was folded so you had to unfold it to see what was on it."

"Yeah well, you always leaving your trash around, so I figured it was something I could throw away."

"Yeah whatever Lani. I'm a grown ass man. I don't have to answer to you. I'm sick of you accusing me of shit and looking for shit. Just say you don't trust me. Cuz you don't and therefore there's no need for us to be together anymore. I'll pack my shit and head back to Connecticut."

"First of all, nobody accused you of anything. But if you want to leave then go ahead motherfucker. I don't even care." And she hung up in his face. Lani didn't even care about what Love was saying. She did not like how he told her he was grown and didn't have to answer to her. *That motherfucker is crazy. He grown he don't have to answer to me. Any grown man know he has to answer to his wife. He grown huh, let me see his grown ass go get a phone in his name. Let me see his grown ass get an apartment in his name. He ain't grown. He a grown ass baby. He kill me wit' that shit, always trying to make me seem like the bad one. All I did was ask him a question. I never accused him of anything. I'm sick of him threatening to leave me. He ain't fucking leaving anyway,* Lani thought.

220

Although Lani never really accused him of anything, she did think he was with a chick, but then she also thought he may have gone to the club or something. Either way, she didn't know; she just wanted to ask him about it and she accepted his answer but he was the one who blew it out of proportion.

Over the next two days, they did not say anything to each other. Lani didn't care either, in a way she wanted him to go back home. The second day, when she went home on her lunch break, Love was on his way out the door. As he was walking out the door, he asked Lani, "What car you want me to leave you?"

"You can take the Acura."

"I'm talking about when I leave for good."

"I know. You can take the Acura." Lani still didn't think he was serious about leaving. When he walked out the door, she called him on the phone. "So when you leaving?" She asked.

"Next week."

"So you just gon' continue to stay here until you leave?"

"Why, you want me out?"

"I'm sayin', ain't no point in you staying here if we not together."

"Alright then, that's cool. I'll go stay with my uncle. I'll pack my bags and shit when I come back in town tomorrow."

"Tomorrow? Where you going?"

"I'm going to handle some business so I can get this money right to get the fuck out of here."

"So that's it? It's over just like that?"

"Yeah because I'm sick of going through this shit with you. Bad enough I'm not happy down here cuz I ain't making no fucking money, but I'm bearing with it to make you happy and it seem like

221

that ain't enough. I'm livin' paycheck to paycheck. I feel like a fuckin' bum. I can't be no average nigga Lani."

"But Love, I didn't accuse you of anything."

"Yeah, but you went searching through my shit and you shouldn't have even asked me about it. Well anyway, I don't want to talk about it."

"What you mean you don't want to talk about it?" Lani asked while on her way outside to talk to him face to face before he pulled off. Love just hung up. She went to the car to finish the conversation. "Why you hang up on me?" Lani asked.

"Because, I told you I don't want to talk about it. There's nothing to talk about."

"Well I feel like you at least owe me an explanation."

"I gave you an explanation. I'm sick of going through this with you. It's a new year. I thought we left the bullshit back at home. Every couple of months I'm going through this shit."

"Well first of all, nobody accused you of anything. You the one who overreacted. I just asked you a simple question, you gave me your answer and I accepted it. That was that."

"You went through my shit. You don't trust me."

"I do trust you. What are you talking about. I can't help how I feel about certain situations though. The shit just didn't look right. It would be no different if I was at work and you thought I was there until six or whatever and you found out I got off at 1:30, you would want to know where I was at too."

"No, no, no. I wouldn't have been searching through your shit in the first place."

"Yeah whatever. You kill me with that shit. You do the same shit I do. The same way you went through my bag and found those letters from Donell."

222

"No, I was looking for some paper to write my man. I saw the letter and I thought it was for me because Wayne told me he would write me and put it in your name."

"Okay, well even still, if that was the case, when you seen it wasn't for you, you still didn't leave it alone."

"Listen man, I'm not gonna talk about it. Let me go on about my business so I can get this money right so I can get the fuck out of here."

"That's your problem. You always want to run from shit. That's all you know how to do is run. That's the shit I'm talking about. It makes no sense for me to be sitting up here giving 110% and you giving 50." At that point, Love banged on the steering wheel enraged with anger as blood rushed to his face.

"What the fuck you mean? I am giving 110%. I'm fucking going to work busting my ass coming home sore as fuck and at the end of the week I ain't making no fucking money. I don't even like it down here but I'm dealing with it because of you. Just let me go, damn. Everytime I want to leave you never let me go, just let me go man." Lani and Love stared at each other for about ten seconds and Lani finally got out the car. She hadn't cried not once up to this point and she still didn't. She let Love go and she went back to work.

While at work, she tried her best to focus on other things, but her mind kept drifting back to the situation at hand. At this point, she knew Love was serious about what he was saying. She didn't think he really wanted to break up with her, but the reason she really thought he was serious was because he wanted to get back home to the streets. She thought he really would leave, make some money, and then try to get back with her. It finally dawned on her that he was going to leave her a thousand miles away from home by herself.

223

While at work, she sent him a text message that read, *I love you and I know you love me. You brought me down here and now you just gon' leave me like that. We've been through way worse shit than this. I know how you feel about everything but please don't leave me down here by myself. Did you forget that you are the only one I have down here?* About an hour later, she called Love. She tried to talk to him and apologized for what she had done, but he had his mind made up – he was leaving.

She wasn't able to function anymore at work and left early. As soon as she reached her apartment door, she burst out crying. Most of her anger was geared toward the fact that she would be lonely. She hadn't planned on going back up north until her lease was up, which was about nine months away. She was also sad that he was breaking up with her, but the most important matter at hand was how she would pay $1500 in bills making $1200. She kicked herself over and over at the fact that she always had to mess something up.

After she talked to Love a second time later and realized he still wasn't letting up, she accepted the fact that he was leaving. His mentality made her more upset because all he wanted to do was hustle. He didn't even care about what happened to them (or her at least) and all the bullshit the streets came with. He was too old to still want to be out there like that. The thought of that made her accept the hurt right then and there in order to be spared the hurt that would come in the future. *Fuck it. Let it be over because the way he going, we not gon' last anyway. He say he don't care if he go to jail, but that's bullshit. He gon' be in there and I'm gon' be out here, so let his ass leave. He gon' be mad as fuck when he in there and I'm out here wit' somebody else. He gon' be made as fuck when I make*

224

it off my book and he gon' wish he would have just chilled. It's all good, Lani thought.

Just when she became content that their relationship was over, Love came home and told her he thought about all that she was saying while he drove home. He told her he would wait until their lease was up to leave. Lani then thought the whole thing was a game and he didn't plan on leaving in the first place; she thought he just wanted to teach her a lesson. Another reason she thought he didn't leave was because he didn't want everyone to get on him about leaving her down there, especially her mother.

Lani promised herself that she would never get involved with a dude who was in the street. She wished she had stayed single. She was at the point in her life where being single would be the best thing for her. She was back in school and whether or not her book brought her success or not, in three years, she would be making $100,000 a year. She was more focused than ever and she could see the vision; being in a relationship only made her less focused. She didn't want to have anyone to think about anymore. Though she loved him with all her heart, she honestly could say she would be content if he walked out her life right then and there. She would be hurt, but as they say, "all wounds heal over time." She was young and felt she could put relationships off until she was thirty.

It wasn't worth all she went through. She had put Love first on a lot of shit and she always kept "them" in mind. He on the other hand, was thinking about himself. She promised she would get her a man who worked so she wouldn't have to worry whether or not he was coming home at night. She knew another man like Love wouldn't come her way, but she did know he would be coming home every night and that she could live with. For the time being, she just let everything flow, whatever happened was going to happen. Love

225

had it set in his mind that he was going back to Connecticut and Lani didn't want to go back there. She was sick of doing what he wanted to do so she was moving to Northern New Jersey or New York, with or without him.

Back at home, things hadn't changed. Lani kept in contact with Nisha and Marie often to catch up on the latest. Deshawn had his daughter but he was back in jail because he and his baby's mother had a fight and she called the cops on him. He and Marie were starting to fall in love with each other and she basically shut Mark out her life. She was still going to see him, but she visited Deshawn more than Mark.

While incarcerated, Deshawn tried to get Marie to be cool with his baby's mother on the strength of his daughter. Lani tried to tell Marie not to do that because once shit got out about them, there would be drama. His baby's mother was Candy's cousin and Lani could hear Candy now, *See I told you about that bitch. She grimy as fuck.* After a while, Marie fell back from her, taking Lani's advice.

Torey was still trying to get in contact with Marie while in jail. Being the bitch he was, he told her if she didn't be with him, he would chaos her and would make sure she wasn't happy. She told him to just leave her alone and go on about his business because there was no need for the two of them to be together. She hated him now and in an effort to hope he would leave her alone for good, she told him he shouldn't be with her because when he found out what she had done (with DeShawn), he wouldn't want to be with her anyway.

Not long after that, Marie told Lani she and Deshawn were moving in together when he got out. "Damn, you just shitted on Mark," Lani told her. Deshawn told her he was leaving his baby's mother and they would be together. Besides, his baby's mother was using him for his money anyway. What type of female writes her man letters in jail asking him to buy her a car for Christmas? She really wanted Marie's mother (who held his money) to give her money to buy a car while he was in jail. She even wanted him to still pay her bills. Any female who cared about her man would be writing him telling him how miserable she was.

Marie wanted to break the news to Mark while he was still in jail, fearing he would beat her ass when he got out. Her plan was to tell him she cheated on him with Torey because he told her if he found out she cheated on him, he would be straight on her; and he meant what he said. She wanted to write him and break up with him, but he wasn't making it any easier by calling her and telling her he loved her. She didn't know what to do. Once again, she had gotten herself in some bullshit.

Like Lani, she too wished she was single so she didn't care what happened at that point. She wanted to live stress free. She had been through too much over the past few years with men and now she wanted to do her. She definitely needed a break from the headaches. Problems she and Lani went through in recent years, also put a strain on their relationship, but they still hung in there with each other.

She ultimately decided to give her relationship with Deshawn a try. While he was incarcerated, she began looking for apartments so they could move in with each other. She liked Deshawn, but deep down inside she wanted to still be with Mark but she knew Mark wasn't stupid and she knew he would keep his word and leave her once he confirmed she cheated with Torey; therefore she chose to be with Shawn. After building her courage, she decided to tell Mark she cheated on him.

She visited him one day and told him she cheated on him with Torey. Mark was not shocked at all but thought she still dealt with Torey; he didn't know Torey was in jail at the time. He told her he wasn't mad and that he been knew. Candy had written him letters about her infidelity and so had Klarissa. He told her he got what he deserved being that he took her from Torey. He told her Torey would never be able to fuck her the way he did and he also told her Torey didn't look better than him. He told her he would be able to fuck her whenever he came home because that pussy would always be his. He told her he would also still come around because he and her mother were cool. They broke up but he reminded her that "she was losing out on some good cock." She was hurt and confused, but she was happy she got her confession out. Because of how he took her confession, she had second thoughts about being with Deshawn because she didn't know what would happen when he came home. She eventually decided to give Deshawn a try because she didn't want Mark to come home and feel he had to get revenge on her.

A few weeks after that, Mark called her and asked her if she had pictures in jail. A friend of his who was transferred to his jail from the same jail Torey was in, told Mark about the naked pictures Torey had of her. Torey found the camera he supposedly "lost" and had his mother develop the pictures and send them to him. He tarnished her reputation and made her life miserable altogether.

Months after Lani moved to Georgia, Niya visited Lani. Being the good friend Lani was, she told Niya she didn't have to waste money on a hotel, she was welcomed to stay with her. She showed her a good time while she was there and Niya even decided to move to GA. Lani was home with Niya four of the five days she was there and worked on the fifth day. She decided to leave work early to

228

spend the final hours with her friend and also bring her to the airport. Niya and Love were home by themselves waiting for Lani to return. They didn't know Lani would be getting off work early, and when Lani walked in the house, she almost died from what she saw.

Niya and Love froze, both speechless. Niya was on top of Love riding him. Any other woman would have blacked out and jumped on both of them instantly. Lani on the other hand, was to the point where she really couldn't get mad at Love anymore because he'd already done enough damage in their relationship. She looked at Niya and said, "Let's go, put your clothes on. I'm bringing you to the airport." Love didn't know what to say and Niya couldn't even look at Lani.

Lani and Niya never made it to the airport. Instead Lani drove about thirty miles from her home to an empty field. She ordered Niya out the car saying she wanted to talk to her.

"I can't even believe you." Lani spoke. Niya's heart was pounding out her chest and she didn't have any words to say. "I brought you in my home yo. I trusted you enough to bring you around my man. I looked out for you like a sister. I would have never done that shit to you yo."

"I really did not intend for that to happen Lani. He was coming at me."

"Oh, and you just couldn't brush him off? You thought I wouldn't find out or something? And you did that shit in my house. You should have called me and told me what the fuck was good."

"I know. I know. I can't even say I'm sorry because that's not going to do anything."

"You damn right it's not." Lani pulled out her gun and pointed it at Niya. "You have any last words to say before you meet your maker?" Niya didn't have anything to say after that. She was fearful and began shedding tears. "No time for crying now. It's too late for that bullshit. Maybe it's my fault. I should have never became friends with you. Maybe Marie was right when she said I shouldn't be bringing other chicks in our circle. She was right, I can't trust other bitches. Bitches are shiesty. I'm better off with me, myself, and I. I can only trust me. I can't even blame you, this is all my fault." Lani then lowered the gun. Niya breathed a sigh of relief. "But fuck that bitch, you violated. Like Love used to always tell me, sometimes people only respect violence. When you be too nice to them, they take advantage of that. I'm sorry, but I gotta make an example out of you."

Lani pulled the trigger, shooting Niya twice in the chest. She didn't even run from the scene, she just drove away like it was nothing. She didn't even care if she was still alive; she just left her there to die. Where she was, no one would find her until days later.

Lani didn't cry one time; she wasted all her tears back at home. When she arrived home, Love dropped to his knees and clutched her legs and begged for forgiveness. He wished in his mind that he could rewind the time and not have cheated on her for the second time and this time with her best friend. "I'm sorry boo, I love you. You are who I want to spend my life with. You are who I have built everything with, not anyone else. You are the one with the ring. Please don't leave me."

"Please don't leave you...please don't fucking leave you? I come home early from work and you in our bed fucking my best friend. What the fuck is wrong with you? Love is irrelevant right now. You don't respect me and you don't love me. I forgave you once. I even forgave you when you burnt me motherfucker. I got guns pointed to my head for you and this is how you repay me? I don't fucking get it. I have been the best fucking woman to you, but I

230

guess that just wasn't enough." Lani exploded. This was the last draw for him. As a woman, you just have to know when enough is enough. You have to know what you can forgive, and what you must not forgive; and Lani could not forgive this. Had it been another woman she didn't know, she still couldn't forgive him because he disrespected the house they resided in.

Love begged and begged for forgiveness. "Baby please. I know I fucked up, but I love you. There's no doubt about that, anyone can see that. Don't do this to me, please."

"Don't do this to you? Don't do this to you? That's all you fucking think about is you. You, you, you. There's more to life than just you motherfucker. You should have thought about me when you laid down with these bitches."

"I did think of you."

"Well what the fuck did you think about? When I was coming home? Or would I find out about this? What did you think? That she, or rather they, were me? You are a fucking disgrace. You walk around all innocent like you not like all these other dudes, when in fact you have been the worst and the best man I have ever been with, now how is that possible?" There was no doubt in her mind that he didn't love her because if there were, she definitely would not have stayed with him the first time. He did truly love her though; they both felt like they were each other's solemate.

He had no idea Lani murdered Niya. He also had no idea what his fate was. "I can't do this shit anymore. I can't stress myself. I'll mess around and die messing with you. I went through this same shit with you over a year ago. You just didn't learn, huh. All the girls in the world and you had to sleep with my friend. What were you thinking? You thought I wouldn't find out again, huh? You are so stupid."

231

She was now on the verge of slapping the shit out him, but she knew what happened the last time she put her hands on him. She knew that if she took him back, he would assume that he could do anything to her and she would put up with it. She couldn't forgive him for what he'd done to her no matter how she felt about him; she would just have to get over it in time. She wished it didn't happen, but she took it as a sign from the almighty Lord that he was not the one for her, no matter what she thought. She also wondered if he even used a condom. From the first incident, she knew that was too risky to forgive again. Niya may have been her friend, but that didn't mean she couldn't have a disease.

"Why you looking at me like that?" He said curiously as she gave him a look like he was her worse enemy. She walked away mumbling. He just sat shaking his head and sighing. Lani walked outside to get her pistol out the car and appeared three minutes later and all he heard was a click/clack sound. She was so upset, she didn't even close the door all the way. He turned around only to see her standing in the doorway with her baby glock.

"I love you baby. I always did. I never cheated on you. I gave you my all but I guess that wasn't good enough. If I can't be with you, nobody can."

"Baby please, don't do this. Think about what you're doing. We can work it out." Unlike before, Love was scared this time. The circumstances were a lot harsher so he knew Lani would probably pull the trigger.

"No, fuck that, we can't work shit out." As tears began rolling down her baby face, she began to think about all the wonderful times they had together. She loved him with all her heart and she knew that no matter how good of a man the next one may be, she knew no one could compare to Love. She also knew she couldn't put the gun

232

down or he would probably kill her for pointing a gun at him. As he inched closer to her, she cocked the gun back and fired a warning shot just past his shoulder. "I'm not fucking playing with you." By this point, she had sparked someone to call 911 citing a strange "boom" sound.

"Yo, what the fuck is wrong with you? Please calm down. It's not worth it."

You thought about that when you was in that pussy? No. So why should I? Any man who fucks his wife's friend, has no respect for his wife. And she the fool anyway for thinking she could possibly take you from me. She don't know she would have just been a piece of ass. Well she's a done deal anyway."

"You don't have to do this. Please baby, please."

"Sorry boo, I love you, but I really can't do this with you anymore."

"Fuck it." He stared at her for about thirty seconds, and then dodged for the gun. *Bang, bang.* He was dead. She shot him in the head twice as he tried to wrestle for the gun and made her nervous. Would she really had shot him? No she wouldn't have; she loved him so much that even if she couldn't or wouldn't be with him anymore, she still wanted to be able to see him. She didn't even cry as she saw him drop.

"Put that gun down ma'am," she heard from behind her. She had no clue the cops were on their way because someone called them when they heard gun shots. She turned around with the gun still in her hand which was now pointing at the cops. They shot her because they thought she was about to shoot them. She dropped right beside LOVE.

Damn Love, you should've had my back.

Epilogue

Lani may have found the love of her life, but was it worth everything she went through to get it, before, during and after? Meeting Love definitely changed her life and made her a better person, but she never thought she would go through such pain to become the woman she was. Love was the best and worst man she ever had; now how is that possible? Although the good outweighed the bad, was it really worth the risk of possibly losing her life? Was it worth losing a close friend; or did her relationship expose her friend for who she really was?

The way everything was put together and flowed with one another, it brings about the theory of fatalism (the belief that everything happens by fate). It was meant for Lani to meet Marie in junior high and become close friends with her; she was just the doorway to meeting her Love. It was meant for her to be a "black girl lost" in the streets so Love could come and pick her up. It was meant for Donell to treat her badly, go to jail, and Love come home a month later to find her. Everything coordinated all too perfectly so no matter how hard she may have tried, she would not have been successful in evading Love. Whether it was him or someone else, God had someone waiting for Lani, she just had other obstacles in her way that she had to overcome before, during, and after him.

Some may say Love is an emotion; some may say it is a choice and you choose what it makes you do. Both may be true, but everyone is destined for this choice or emotion. You definitely choose what it makes you do, but this emotion and feeling can vary from person to person, and depending on how it affects you, your actions may be uncontrollable. It can take you out of your character and you may really have to sit back, collect your thoughts and say, *what the hell is wrong with me*? Just think about it, how often do you hear on the news about someone who killed their mate because they cheated on them? Even though Lani didn't kill Love and didn't get shot by the police, these events are very common, mostly ending in a murder-suicide. Before entering a relationship, you just have to be the person who loves yourself more than any one else. You cannot give love if you do not love yourself first, if you try, your relationship will be disastrous.

Certain events in life, one should always expect the worst because if you are expecting the best, when something bad happens, it will devastate you; whereas if you had expected the worst and some good comes out the situation, you will not be hurt, but rather joyous of the outcome. Life is a big game that we are all playing, some may play it well, some may lose, but the game of life can be very challenging. Bad times are guaranteed and so are good times, but bad times last longer. God will never give you anything you can't handle, but don't get it twisted, you can definitely get yourself in situations you cannot handle; as the saying goes, "if it doesn't kill you, it only makes you stronger." As long as you stay positive and believe things will get better, you will survive. Like other things in life, being hurt by love is not the end of the world. It is only a test and a lesson. Many female musicians have turned their pain into love and became successful, proving you can turn negative events into positive outcomes.

All men are the same regardless of what one may think. You can be the best woman possible to a man, but that is never enough. Don't think it is anything with you, always have enough self-esteem and confidence to say nothing is wrong with you; it's just almost impossible for a man to be faithful. You can either deal with it or not; but don't think if you dump one man and go to the next that he will be different. If you choose to deal with a man, make sure he treats you right and doesn't treat you anything less than what you deserve. If not, then you must move on to someone who is willing to do that for you, otherwise, you're selling yourself short of what you are worth.

Not many women can deal with a man who cheats. That leaves you wondering, is it worth staying with him in order to avoid being alone or is it best to deal with the inevitable pain of loneliness? Only you can decide what best suits your need, but whatever you decide, just know you chose to do that. Before you even involve yourself in a relationship, make sure you are independent and can survive without that man; otherwise you will be with him for all the wrong reasons.

What men don't realize is that women are the originators of cheating and we have more game; so there is really nothing they can do to get over on us. Think about it, how often do men cheat and get caught versus how often women cheat and get caught. As with Lani's situation, she could have cheated on Love with Donell and never got caught. The only way he would have known would have been from her confessing as she did. She wrote him and visited him numerous times before Love found the letters; whereas Love cheated on her and was caught the very same night. A woman has more game and power than a man; our only problem is that we wear our emotions on our sleeve. We have something powerful, but we don't use it correctly; if we did, we would have them eating out the palm of our hand. Any man will confess that we have the upper hand on many situations; we just don't take advantage of that.

Love is impossible to avoid. If ever you should encounter Love, be smart, keep your eyes open and stay on your toes. Do not let anyone use and abuse you, put your foot down and do not accept anything less than what you are worth. If you give your all and it still fails, do not get frustrated, just hold your head high and understand that shit happens and most of the time it happens for a reason. Forgive and forget certain things, but know when to draw the line, don't let a man think he can do anything to you and get away with it.

While you are in a relationship, there are many things you should abide by. First and foremost, DO NOT involve ANYONE in your relationship. As with Lani, involving other people in her relationship was not a good idea, it only made her relationship worse. I don't care if it is your best friend and you tell her everything, do not do it. If you and your mate have a problem, work it out together because only the two of you know about your relationship. Secondly, give your all, if you are not willing to be in it for the long haul, then don't be in it. Let the person know from the very beginning what your intentions are.

Honesty is another quality your relationship should have. You should be honest from the very moment you meet someone. When you lie, you have to make up multiple lies to cover the previous lie and after a while you forget your lies, and eventually the other person will think you are lying about everything thereafter. You don't want to be accused of lying each and every time, especially when you know you are telling the truth. Tell the truth even if you think it may hurt the other person. If you don't want to hurt them, then don't do anything you may feel you need to lie about to spare their feelings; because remember, what's in the dark always comes to light. Relationships are always bad when there is no trust. The three important things to making a relationship last include but are not limited to –

Commitment first, then Trust, and finally Love. Finally, ladies, DO NOT stay with a man who beats on you. No matter how many times they say they won't do it again, they will and eventually you will end up dead; if he beats on you, he does not love you – stop making excuses for him.

And always remember, there is someone great out there for you, but your prince charming is not married and is not involved with someone else, he is single for you and only you. Too often, and not just with infidelity, women involve themselves with a man who tells them his situation from the beginning and usually what he is looking for and not looking for; but the female still deals with him thinking she could change him and get upset when she catches feelings and he isn't willing to change. If that's what he said from the beginning and you know you are not looking for that, then don't involve yourself with him; and not just women, men do it too, you're only setting yourself up for unnecessary pain in the future that could have been avoided.

Never get involved with someone who is in a relationship and definitely not a married man. You are only setting yourself up for disaster; if he did it to her, he will do it to you, never think you are any different than the next woman. Never accept being second to any other female. Besides, no matter what he tells you, he is not leaving his wife; so you becoming emotionally involved would be pointless. He does not love you; you are only there for his own pleasure. There are other men out there who are single and willing to give you everything. Avoid love triangles; they only end in pain, either physically or emotionally. Only you can make your choices in life, but remember, you've been warned. No one can teach you about relationships except experience. There's nothing wrong with advice, that's what it's there for, but don't take anything if they're advising you to do it. Make your own decisions to receive your own consequence or reward.

Printed in the United States
121783LV00003B/34/A